WY PLAY HOUSE

Electricity
By **Murray Gold**

Company

Christopher Eccleston	Jakey
Patrick Brennan	Leo
Oliver Wood	Bizzy
Sophie Ward	Katherine
Andrew Scarborough	Michael

First performance:
Courtyard Theatre, West Yorkshire Playhouse, 26 March 2004

West Yorkshire Playhouse
Playhouse Square
Quarry Hill
Leeds
LS2 7UP
0113 213 7700
www.wyp.org.uk

Director	**Ian Brown**
Designer	**Ruari Murchison**
Lighting Designer	**Tim Mitchell**
Composer	**Richard Taylor**
Sound Design	**Mic Pool**
Dialect Coach	**Penny Dyer**
Fight Director	**Renny Krupinski**
Voice	**Susan Stern**
Assistant Director	**Sarah Punshon**
Casting	**Kay Magson**
Deputy Stage Manager	**Rhian Thomas**

Production Thanks
Furniture 123 Limited, 0113 248 2233,
www.furniture123.co.uk
subway

THERE WILL BE ONE INTERVAL OF FIFTEEN MINUTES

BSL interpreted performance: Wednesday 14 April 7.45pm
BSL interpreter: Alan Haythornthwaite

Audio described performances: Friday 16 & Tuesday 20 April
7.45pm & Thursday 22 April 2pm
Audio described by Anne Muers and Pam Wells

Captioned performance: Monday 19 April 7.45pm
Captioned by Pat Collcutt

Smoking in the auditorium is not permitted. The use of cameras and
recording equipment is strictly prohibited. Please ensure that mobile
phones, pagers and digital alarm watches are SWITCHED OFF before
you enter the auditorium.

CAST

Christopher Eccleston Jakey

Born in Salford and trained at Central School of Speech and Drama
Theatre credits include: *Hamlet* (West Yorkshire Playhouse); *Miss Julie*
(Haymarket Theatre); *Encounters* (Royal National Theatre Studio);
Abingdon Square, *Bent* (Royal National Theatre); *Dona Rosita*, *A
Streetcar Named Desire* (Bristol Old Vic);
Television credits include: *Cracker*, *Hearts and Minds*, *Our Friends in
the North*, *Hillsborough*, *Clocking Off*, *Othello*, *Sunday*, *The King and
Us*, *The League of Gentlemen*, *Flesh and Blood*, *Second Coming*.
Film credits include: *Let Him Have It* (Vivid); *Shallow Grave* (Figment
Films); *Jude* (Polygram); *Elizabeth* (Working Title); *The Others*
(Sogecine SA); *24 Hour Party People* (Revolution Films); *28 Days Later*
(DNA).

Patrick Brennan Leo

Trained: Central School of Speech and Drama.
Theatre credits include: *Macbeth*, *Don Juan* (West Yorkshire Playhouse);
Richard II, *Edward II*, *Twelfth Night*, *Macbeth* (Shakespeare's Globe);
Light Shining in Buckinghamshire, *Schism in England*, *Entertaining
Strangers*, *Antony and Cleopatra*, *King Lear* (National Theatre); *A
Clockwork Orange*, *Romeo and Juliet*, *Hamlet* (RSC); *Outside Edge*
(New Vic, Staffs); *Fire Eaters* (Actors Centre); *The Tempest* (Derby
Playhouse); *King Lear*, *Richard III*, *The Taming of the Shrew* (Ludlow
Festival); *Fire Raisers*, *Casement* (Moving Theatre); *Glengarry
Glenross*, *Absurd Person Singular* (Wolsey Theatre, Ipswich); *I am
Joseph Stalin* (White Bear, Kennington); *Under Milk Wood* (Bristol Old
Vic); *Worlds Apart* (Theatre Royal Stratford East); *Twelfth Night*
(Thorndike Theatre, Leatherhead); *The Merchant of Venice* (Sherman
Theatre, Cardiff); *Threepenny Opera* (Hi Jinx, Cardiff); *Best Years of
Our Lives* (Made in Wales, Cardiff); *Song From a Forgotten City* (Y
Cwmni, Cardiff); *Crimes of the Heart* (Phoenix Arts, Leicester); *King
Lear*, *Some Kind of Hero* (Nottingham Playhouse); *Silicon Alley*
(Nottingham Roundabout); *The Hairy Ape* (Octagon Theatre, Bolton).
Television credits include: *Cadfael*, *Wing and a Prayer*, *The Bill*,
Midsomer Murders, *Every Cloud*, *Nightshift*, *Brothers and Members*,
Order Out of Chaos, *In The Company of Strangers*, *Holby City*, *Without
Motive*, *State of Play* and the BBC and Globe live broadcast of
Richard II.
Radio credits include numerous broadcasts for BBC Radio 3, 4 and
Wales.

Oliver Wood Bizzy

Trained: Royal Welsh College of Music and Drama.
Theatre credits include: *Romeo and Juliet* (English Touring Theatre);
Speakeasy (Sherman Theatre, Cardiff); *Mill on the Floss*, *Some Voices*,
Assassins (Bute Theatre, Cardiff); *What the Butler Saw* (Caird Theatre,
Cardiff); *Woyzeck* (Fuceccio, Italy); *Pendragon* (The Minac Theatre);
Mystery Bouffe (Theatr Brycheiniog, Brecon).

Sophie Ward Katherine

Theatre credits include: *Nothing, Venice Preserv'd, Three Sisters, Semi
Monde. Blithe Spirit, Les Liaisons Dangereuses, Turn of the Screw, The
Robbers, Hamlet, Don Carlos, The Milk Train, Private Lives* and *Flare
Path* (Citizens' Theatre).
Television credits include: *Dinotopia, Legacy, A Village Affair, Chiller:
Prophecy, Taking Liberty, Dark Adapted Eye, MacGyver: Atlantis, Class
of '61, Events at Drimaghleen, The Strauss Dynasty, Miss Marple, The
Shell Seekers, A Time of Indifference, Casanova, Too Old to Fight* and
Frost in May.
Film credits include: *Dead in the Water, Bella Donna, The Big Fall,
Crime and Punishment, Wuthering Heights, The Monk, A Demon in my
View, Benevenuto Cellini, Young Toscanini, A Summer Story, Little
Dorrit, Aria, Young Sherlock Holmes, Return to Oz* and *A Shocking
Accident.*

Andrew Scarborough Michael

Theatre credits include: *The Master Builder* (Albery Theatre); *Wild
Orchids* (Chichester Festival Theatre); *Handbag* (ATC); *Wuthering
Heights* (Good Company); *Loot* (Theatre Clwyd); *Hamlet* (Almeida
Theatre/Tour); *Wuthering Heights* (Theatre Royal, York); *A Midsummer
Night's Dream*, *Government Inspector* (Harrogate Theatre); *Henry V*
(Tabard).
Television credits include: *Hearts and Bones, The Innocent, Heartbeat,
The Bill, Casualty, Dangerfield, Touching Evil, Silent Witness, Trial and
Retribution* and *Streets of Gold.*
Film credits include: *Jason and the Argonauts* and *The Sax Man.*

CREATIVES

Murray Gold Writer

Murray Gold was born in Portsmouth in 1969.
Plays include *50 Revolutions* (Whitehall Theatre, London 2000, dir
Dominic Dromgoole); *Candide* (The Gate Theatre, London 1997, dir
David Farr); *Resolution* (BAC, 1994, dir David Farr). He won the
Michael Imison Memorial Prize for Radio Drama in 2001.
As composer, Murray was awarded the Mozart de la Septième Art award
in France (2003) for his score to Emily Young's feature film *Kiss of Life*.
He has written music for many television shows including *Shameless*,
The Second Coming, *Queer as Folk*, *The Canterbury Tales*, *Vanity Fair*,
Servants and *Clocking Off*.

Ian Brown Director

Ian Brown is Artistic Director and Chief Executive of the West Yorkshire
Playhouse, where he has directed *The Wind in the Willows, A Small
Family Business, Pretending to be Me, Hamlet, The Lady in the Van,
Hijra, Eden End, Stepping Out, Broken Glass, The Comedy of Errors,
Proposals, You'll Have Had Your Hole* and *Of Mice and Men*.
Theatre credits include: *Equus* (Beer Sheva Theatre, Israel); *Goodnight
Children Everywhere*, which won the Olivier Award for Best New Play,
Victoria (RSC); *Five Kinds of Silence* (The Lyric, Hammersmith);
Strangers on a Train (Colchester, Guildford and Richmond); *Babycakes*
(Drill Hall); *Food for Love* (Donmar Warehouse); *Widows* (Traverse
Theatre, Edinburgh); *Steaming* (Piccadilly Theatre); *Nabokov's Gloves*
(Hampstead Theatre); *Killing Rasputin* (Bridewell Theatre); the original
production of *Trainspotting* (Citizens' Theatre and The Bush Theatre).
From 1988 to 1999 Ian was Artistic Director and Executive Director of
the Traverse Theatre, Edinburgh. Productions included: *Reader, The
Collection, Unidentified Human Remains and the True Nature of Love*
and *Poor Super Man* (Evening Standard Award), *Ines de Castro, Light
in the Village, Moscow Stations* with Tom Courtenay (Evening Standard
Award, Best Actor), *Hanging the President* (Scotsman Fringe First), *The
Bench, Hardie and Baird, Bondagers* (which transferred to the Donmar
Warehouse and World Stage Festival, Toronto), *Shining Souls*.
Ian was also Artistic Director of TAG Theatre Company, Citizens' Theatre
for five years, where productions included: *Othello, A Midsummer
Night's Dream, As You Like It, Romeo and Juliet, Hard Times, Can't
Pay? Won't Pay!, Great Expectations.*
Ian trained as a teacher at The Central School of Speech and Drama and
spent five years teaching in Stoke Newington and at The Cockpit Theatre,
London.

Ruari Murchison Designer

Has designed productions at Washington DC, Stuttgart (Germany),
Luzern (Switzerland), Holland, Denmark and The Stratford Festival
(Canada). London work includes productions at the National Theatre,
Royal Court, Young Vic, Hampstead Theatre Club, Drill Hall, Soho

Theatre, Greenwich Theatre, Royal Opera House and for the Royal Shakespeare Company. He has worked in major regional theatres including Nottingham Playhouse, Crucible Theatre Sheffield, West Yorkshire Playhouse, Theatr Clwyd, Birmingham Rep, Birmingham Royal Ballet and Bristol Old Vic.

Recent design work includes: *Titus Andronicus* (Royal Shakespeare Company); *Mappa Mundi, Frozen, The Waiting Room, The Red Balloon* (National Theatre); *Henry IV* Parts 1 and 2 (Washington DC); *A Busy Day* (Lyric Theatre,Shaftsbury Avenue); *Peggy Sue Got Married* (Shaftesbury Theatre); *The Snowman* (Peacock Theatre); *Gone to L.A.* (Hampstead Theatre); *West Side Story, The Sound of Music* (Stratford Festival, Canada); *Hamlet* (Elisnore, Denmark); *Medea* (West Yorkshire Playhouse); *A Doll's House, The David Hare Trilogy – Racing Demon, Absence of War, Murmuring Judges* – TMA Best Design Nomination, *The Tempest, Macbeth, The Merchant of Venice, Hamlet, Frozen, The Four Alice Bakers, Jumpers, Nativity, Translations, Big Maggie, Playing by the Rules, A Wedding Story* (Birmingham Rep); *Mrs Warren's Profession, The Threepenny Opera, An Enemy of the People* (Theatr Clwyd),

National tours of *Twelfth Night, Hamlet, Merchant of Venice, Romeo and Juliet, A Wedding Story. A Doll's House.*

Opera work includes: *Peter Grimes, Cosi fan Tutte* (Luzerner Opera, Switzerland); *La Cenerentola, Il Barbiere di Siviglia* (Garsington); *L'Italiana in Algeri* (Buxton); *Les Pelerins de la Mecque, ZaZa* (Wexford); *The Magic Flute, A Midsummer Night's Dream* (Covent Garden Festival).

Ballet work includes: *Landschaft und Erinnerung* (Stuttgart Ballett, Germany); *The Protecting Veil* (Birmingham Royal Ballet); *Le Festin de l'Araignee* (Royal Ballet School – Royal Opera House Gala), all choreographed by David Bintley.

Richard Taylor Composer

Richard is currently Music Creator in Residence at the West Yorkshire Playhouse, funded by the PRS Foundation.

Theatre credits include: *Medea, Spring and Port Wine, Single Spies, Enjoy* (West Yorkshire Playhouse); *Humble Boy, Tom's Midnight Garden* (winner TMA Equity Award), *Beauty and the Beast, Molly Sweeney, Death of a Salesman, Arcadia, Philip Pullman's Puss In Boots, The Doll's House, Love! Valour! Compassion!, Communicating Doors, The BFG* (Library Theatre, Manchester); *The Borrowers* (UK tour), *Charlotte's Web* (Library Theatre/Watershed Productions); *The Tinderbox* (Theatre Gwent); *Beauty and the Beast, The Borrowers* (Polka Theatre); *The Tempest* (Contact Theatre, Manchester); *The Provok'd Wife* (Oxford Stage Company); *Metamorphosis* (Everyman Theatre, Cheltenham).

Opera and Musical Theatre credits include: *The Ghosts of Scrooge* (Library Theatre, Manchester); *Corridors* (English National Opera Baylis); *Waiting For Jack, Saints And Singers* (ENO Studio); *Creation* (ETA commission for St. Edmundsbury Cathedral and cathedral tour, including St Mary's Edinburgh, Edinburgh Festival 2002 and Aberdeen International Festival 2002); *The Silver Sword* (Polka Theatre); *Sea Stories* (Theatre Royal, Portsmouth); *Arabian Nights* (Everyman

Theatre, Cheltenham); *Warchild* (National Youth Music Theatre); *A Bao A Qu* (Royal College of Music); *Whistle Down the Wind* (Edinburgh, Sadler's Wells and tour).
Film and television credits include: *Brides in the Bath* (Granada/YTV); *Father Christmas and the Missing Reindeer* (Cosgrove Hall Films/ Anglia TV).
Radio credits include: *Hemlock and After* (BBC Radio 4); *In Company with Sondheim* (BBC Radio 2); *In Tune* (BBC Radio 3); *Loose Ends* (BBC Radio 4).

Tim Mitchell Lighting Designer

Theatre includes *Henry IV* Parts 1 and 2 (Washington); *Of Mice and Men*, *Sweet Panic*, *Benefactors* (West End); *The Play What I Wrote* (Broadway/West End/Tour); *Noises Off* (Broadway/West End/Tour/RNT); *A Doll's House* (Birmingham Rep/Tour); *Hamlet* (Japan/Sadler's Wells); *Piaf*, *A Chorus Line*, *High Society*, *Richard III*, *Edward II* (Crucible Theatre, Sheffield); *A Lie of the Mind*, *Merrily We Roll Along* (Donmar); *Hamlet* (Denmark); *Hand in Hand* (Hampstead Theatre); *The Pajama Game* (Toronto/West End); *The Red Balloon*, *The Alchemist* (RNT); and *The Snowman* (Peacock Theatre). His many other Birmingham Rep shows include *The Atheist's Tragedy* (Gold Medal 1995 Prague Quadrennial), *The Wind in the Willows* and *Hamlet*.
He also works regularly with the RSC including *Othello* (and Japan); *Measure for Measure*, *Taming of the Shrew* (and Washington with *A Tamer Tamed*), *Richard III*, *Titus Andronicus*, as well as *Henry IV* Parts I & II (Olivier Award nomination); *Antony and Cleopatra*, *Much Ado About Nothing*, *The Lieutenant of Inishmore* (all West End transfers), *Macbeth* (transfer Young Vic).
Opera and Ballet: *Die Fledermaus* (WNO); *The Marriage of Figaro*, *Requiem Ballet*, *Don Giovanni* (Kammeroper Vienna); *The Yeomen of the Guard* (D'Oyly Carte); *Carmen Negra* (Icelandic Opera); *Prometheus* (Berlin Philharmonic Orchestra); *On the Town* (LSO).
Tim was lighting designer on *Hamlet* and *A Small Family Business* at the Playhouse and on their co-production of *A View from the Bridge* with Birmingham Rep.
Future plans include *King Lear* (RSC), *Whistling Psyche* (Almeida) and *Ariadne auf Naxos* (WNO).

Mic Pool Sound Designer

In a twenty-seven year career in theatre sound Mic has been resident at the Lyric Theatre Hammersmith, the Royal Court Theatre, Tyne Theatre Company and toured internationally with Ballet Rambert. He has designed the sound for over 300 productions including more than 150 for the West Yorkshire Playhouse where he is currently Director of Creative Technology. He received a TMA award in 1992 for Best Designer (Sound) for *Life Is A Dream* and was nominated for both the Lucille Lortel and the Drama Desk Award for Outstanding Sound Design 2001 for the New York production of *The Unexpected Man*.
Recent theatre credits include: *Brand* (RSC and Haymarket Theatre, London); *Pretending To Be Me* (West Yorkshire Playhouse and West End); *Art* (West End, Broadway and worldwide); *Shockheaded Peter*

(Cultural Industry world tour and West End); *The Unexpected Man* (West End and Broadway); *Beauty and the Beast, A Midsummer Night's Dream, The Seagull, Victoria, Romeo and Juliet, Twelfth Night* and *The Late Shakespeare Plays* at The Roundhouse (RSC); *Hamlet, Four Nights in Knaresborough, The Accrington Pals, The Madness of George III, Two Tracks and Text Me, Blues in the Night* (West Yorkshire Playhouse); *Homage to Catalonia* (West Yorkshire Playhouse, Northern Stage, Teatre Romea, Forum Barcelona 2004 and MC93 Bobigny).

Penny Dyer Dialect Coach

Penny has worked freelance in her profession for 20 years. Other work with Ian Brown includes: *Five Kinds of Silence* (The Lyric, Hammersmith); *Broken Glass*; *The Lady in the Van* (West Yorkshire Playhouse). Recent Theatre includes: for the Donmar - *After Miss Julie*; *The Little Foxes*; *Three Days of Rain*; *The Blue Room* with Nicole Kidman; *Suddenly Last Summer*. For the Almeida - *The Mercy Seat*; *I.D.*; *Camera Obscura*; *The Shape of Things*. For Hampstead Theatre - *Us and Them*; *After the Gods*; *The Lucky Ones*; *The Dead-Eye Boy*; *Buried Alive*. For the Royal Court - *The People are Friendly*; *Plasticine*; *Redundant*; *Spinning into Butter*; *Fireface*. West End – *Happy Days*; *Skellig* at the Young Vic; *A Woman of No Importance*; *Of Mice and Men*; *Ragtime*; *Cat on a Hot Tin Roof*; *A Long Day's Journey into Night*. *The Modernists* (Crucible Theatre, Sheffield); *American Buffalo* (Royal Exchange Theatre, Manchester).
Film & TV credits include: *The Deal*; *Dirty, Pretty Things* (both directed by Stephen Frears); Steve Coogan in *The Alibi*; *Ladies in Lavender*; *Millions*; *The Undertow* with Jamie Bell; *Grass* (BBC); *Peter Pan*; Oliver Parker's *The Importance of Being Earnest*; Tim Roth's *The War Zone*; *Daniel Deronda*; *Plain Jane*; *Anna Karenina*; *Take a Girl Like You*; *The Sleeper*; *The Secret World of Michael Fry*; *The Beach*; the award-winning *Elizabeth*; *Felicia's Journey*; *Oscar and Lucinda*; *The Mask of Zorro*; *The Passion*; *Band of Gold*; *Immortal Beloved*; *The Englishman who went up a Hill*; *Bhaji on the Beach*. Penny has recently completed filming *Piccadilly Jim*, directed by John McKay.

Renny Krupinski Fight Director

Renny Krupinski is a British Equity Registered Fight Director, award-winning actor, writer and director. Theatre fights include: *Ariel* (Dublin); all fights for 2001-2004 seasons at the Royal Exchange & Library Theatres, Manchester; *Macbeth* and *Gagarin Way* (Belfast); *Popcorn* (Liverpool); *Romeo and Juliet* (Clywd); *Les Misérables* (first UK tour, Germany, Belgium), *The Wind in the Willows* and *A Small Family Business* (West Yorkshire Playhouse). TV fights include: *The Bill, City Central, Elidor, A&E, Emmerdale, Brookside, Hollyoaks, Peak Practice* and all the violence for *Coronation Street* over the past two years. Television acting includes: *The Falklands Play, Beech is Back, City Central,* Sizzler in *Brookside, Elidor, Just Us, Silent Witness* and *A Touch of Frost*.
Theatre includes: Salieri/*Amadeus* (twice), Capulet/*Romeo and Juliet*, Banquo/*Macbeth*, Launcelot Gobbo/*Merchant of Venice*.

Directing includes: *Romeo and Juliet*, *Bare*, *The Comedy of Errors*, *Titus Andronicus*, *Arabian Nights*.

Writing includes: *Bare* (International Mobil Playwriting award), *D'Eon, Katie Crowder, Lady Macbeth Rewrites the Rulebook, The Bill* for three years and many BBC Radio comedies.

Recently, Renny filmed *A Touch of Frost* playing Frank Wills and directed and starred in his own plays *Katie Crowder* and *Bare* with his own theatre company Ithaka. He toured his all-female company Broads with Swords in his play *Lady Macbeth Rewrites the Rulebook*. He has just completed a tour of *Bare* with his theatre company Ithaka which, as well as being fight choreographer, writer, director he also starred in.

Susan Stern Voice

Susan trained at the Central School of Speech and Drama and works as an acting teacher, director, writer, text specialist and theatre voice coach. Through her company *Voiceworks* she works on all aspects of voice and performance with clients in theatre, television, radio, education, drama therapy, the professions and business.

Theatre credits include:, *Medea, Hamlet, The Comedy of Errors, A Small Family Business, Playhouse Creatures, Larkin With Women, Kes, Mister Heracles, Eden End* (West Yorkshire Playhouse); *You'll Have Had Your Hole* (West Yorkshire Playhouse/Newcastle Playhouse); *V, The Ballroom of Romance, Animal Farm, A Clockwork Orange* (Newcastle Playhouse); *Trojan Women, Antigone* (Actors of Dionysus); *Shirley Valentine; Man of the Moment, Romeo and Juliet, Othello, Kafka's Dick, Closer, A Midsummer Night's Dream, Dead Funny, Educating Rita* (Theatre Royal, York); *Lord of the Flies, Rumblefish, Road* (Pilot Theatre Company).

Writing credits include: *For the Love of Strangers, Smooth as Chocolate* (BBC Radio 4).

Sarah Punshon Assistant Director

Trained: Royal Scottish Academy of Music and Drama.

Sarah is a Trainee Director at the West Yorkshire Playhouse under the Channel 4 Theatre Director Scheme where her credits as Assistant Director include *The Wind in the Willows* and *The Madness of George III*. This season, Sarah will also be directing *Coming Around Again* at the Playhouse.

Directing credits include: Tony Harrison's *Agamemnon* and Peter Barnes' *Nobody Here But Us Chickens* (RSAMD); Howard Barker's *Judith* (Fitzpatrick Theatre, Cambridge/Stephen Joseph Theatre, Scarborough); Agatha Christie's *The Secret Adversary* (Camden People's Theatre/Bedlam Theatre, Edinburgh Fringe; also co-writer); *Falling Apart* and *The Odyssey* (Perth Youth Theatre); *Tomorrow Unknown* (devised with a group of asylum-seekers for the Scottish Refugee Council).

Assistant Director credits include: *The Good Life* (Tron Theatre, Glasgow); *The Tempest* and *Kabuki-Titus* (Glasgow Repertory Company); *Kill the Old Torture their Young* (RSAMD).

ARTS FOR ALL AT WEST YORKSHIRE PLAYHOUSE

Since opening in 1990, West Yorkshire Playhouse has established a reputation both nationally and internationally as one of Britain's most exciting and active producing theatres, winning awards for everything from its productions to its customer service. The Playhouse provides both a thriving focal point for the communities of West Yorkshire and theatre of the highest standard for audiences throughout the region and beyond. It produces up to 16 of its own shows each year in its two auditoria and stages over 1,000 performances, workshops, readings and community events, watched by over 250,000 people. Alongside this work on stage the Playhouse has an expansive and groundbreaking programme of education and community initiatives and is engaged in the development of culturally diverse art and artists.

A high profile portfolio of international theatre, new writing for the stage, major productions with leading artists and collaborations with some of Britain's brightest touring theatre companies has kept the Playhouse constantly in the headlines and at the forefront of the arts scene. Productions that have made successful transfers to London's West End include *Pretending to be Me*, Tom Courtenay's affectionate tribute to Philip Larkin, *Dangerous Corner* and *Smoking with Lulu*. Our Olivier Award-winning production of Singin' in the Rain completed a UK tour in 2002 following two successful residencies at the Royal National Theatre. 2004 brings together a number of exciting collaborations. As well as Teatre Romea and Northern Stage we are also working on *Vodou Nation* with UK Arts International – a project created in Haiti and touring nationally – and *Batboy The Musical*, a co-production that originates from America and will hopefully find a future life in the UK.

Casting
Kay Magson Casting Director

Company and Stage Management
Diane Asken Company Manager
Paul Veysey and Sarah Northcott Stage Managers
Nina Dilley and Rhian Thomas Deputy Stage Managers
Christine Guthrie and Zoë Taylor-Smith Assistant Stage Managers

Customer Services
Kathy Dean Reception Manager
Leigh Exley and Sangeeta Chana Receptionists

Finance
Teresa Garner Finance Manager
Coleen Anderson Finance Officer
Jenny Copley Cashier
Sadie Bostridge Payroll Officer
Fran Major Ledger Clerk

Housekeeping
Mary Ambrose, Eddy Dube, Michaela Singleton, Teresa Singleton, Sarah Wonnacott and Mike Hilton Cleaners*

Maintenance
Frank Monaghan Maintenance Manager
Tony Proudfoot and Martin McHugh* Maintenance Assistants
Paul Robinson Dayman

Marketing and Sales
Nick Boaden Marketing Manager
Angela Robertson Sales Development Manager
Duncan Grant Graphic Design Manager
Sarah Kennedy Senior Marketing Officer
Simon Bedford Marketing Officer
Aimee Green* Graphic Design Officer
Caroline Gornall Sales Manager
Lynn Hudson, Mel Worman and Bronia Daniels Duty Supervisors
Maureen Kershaw, Sarah Jennings, Rachael Margrave, Dena Marsh, Paul Margrave, Cathryn Taylor, Josie Hoy, Neil Hollingworth and Adele Keating Box Office Assistants

New Writing
Alex Chisholm Literary and Events Manager
Clare Duffy Pearson Writer in Residence
Anita Franklin BBC Writer in Residence

Paint Shop
Virginia Whiteley Head Scenic Artist

Performance Staff
Andy Charlesworth and Jon Murray Firemen
Nathanya Laurent, Shaun Exley, Simon Howarth, Hayley Mort, Jo Murray, Soazig Nicholson, Daneill Whyles, Jemal Cohen, Sangeeta Chana, Andrew Ashdown, Deborah Hargreave, Fiona Heseltine, Monisha Roy, Lewis Smith, Holly Thomas, Rebeka Wilkes, Leigh Exley, Charmaine Jenkins, Sarah Cullen, Victoria Long, Daisy Babbington, Helen West, Chris Clynes, Alison Goodison, Andrew Bramma, Laura Wilkinson, Alan Mawson, Sarah Braithwaite, Averil Fredericks and Rachel Fredericks Attendants*

Press
Rachel Coles Head of Press
Leonie Osborne Press Officer

Production Electricians
Matt Young Chief Electrician
Christopher Sutherland Deputy Chief Electrician
Melani Nicola, Deborah Joyce and Jason Hackett Electricians

Production Management
Suzi Cubbage Production Manager
Eddie de Pledge Production Manager
Christine Alcock Production Administrator

Props Department
Chris Cully Head of Props
Scott Thompson, Susie Cockram and Sarah Partridge Prop Makers

Restaurant and Bar
Charles Smith Food and Beverage Manager
Michael Montgomery Sous Chef
Louise Poulter Chef de Partie
Linda Monaghan Commis Chef
Lee Moran and Lee Dennell Kitchen Porters
Caron Hawley and Esther Lewis Kitchen Assistants
Diana Kendall and Paulene Wilkes-Ruan Restaurant Supervisors
Kath Langton and Gemma Voller Restaurant Assistants
Sarah Allen, Charlene Kendall, Victoria Burt, Ruth Baxter, Jimmy Dunbar, Emma Harrison, Lee Dennell and Emma Litherland Catering Assistants*
Sally Thomas Bar Supervisor
Graeme Thompson and Jo Ash Assistant Bar Supervisors*

Hannah Thomas, Graeme Randall, Nicki Tasker, Jenny Hancock, Anna Alcock, Alice Elerby and Oliver Lord Bar Assistants*

Schools Touring Company
Gail McIntyre Director
Ysanne-Marie Morton Touring and Projects Co-ordinator
John Barber Actor/Puppeteer
Tom Kirkpatrick Composer/Musician

Security
Denis Bray Security Manager and Darkside Security

Sound Department
Glen Massam Head of Sound
Martin Pickersgill Deputy Head of Sound
Selena Davies Sound Technician

Technical Stage Management
Martin S Ross Technical Stage Manager
Michael Cassidy Deputy Technical Stage Manager
Julian Brown Stage Technician

Theatre Operations
Helen Child Head of Operations
Karen Johnson Theatre Manager
Sheila Howarth, Jeni Douglas and Jonathan Dean Duty Managers*

Wardrobe Department
Stephen Snell Head of Wardrobe
Victoria Marzetti Deputy Head of Wardrobe
Julie Ashworth Head Cutter
Nicole Martin Cutter
Alison Barrett Costume Prop Maker/Dyer
Catherine Lowe Wardrobe Assistant
Anne-Marie Hewitt Costume Hire Manager
Kim Freeland Wig and Make-up Supervisor
Catherine Newton Wardrobe Maintenance/ Head Dresser
Paul Worsnop, Katherine Beale and Sarah Wyment Work Experience

*Denotes part-time

West Yorkshire Playhouse Corporate Supporters

Sponsors of the Arts Development Unit

Production Sponsors

Blues in the night

A Small Family Business

The Wind in the Willows

DIRECTORS CLUB

Executive Level Members

Associate Level Members

Director Level Members

Baker Tilly
Cobbetts Solicitors
Crowne Plaza Leeds
GNER
GVA Grimley
Hiscox

Kingston Communications
Provident Financial
The BWB Partnership
Thompson Design
Yorkshire Dales Ice Cream

One Performance Sponsors

O₂
Little Shop of Horrors

Feeling Good Theatre Company
The Elves and the Shoemakers

If you would like to learn how your organisation can become involved with the success of the West Yorkshire Playhouse please contact the Corporate Affairs Department on 0113 213 7275 or email networking@wyp.org.uk

West Yorkshire Playhouse gratefully acknowledges support from

New Opportunities Fund
SPARK and Cyber Cafe

BBC
Northern Exposure

Arts & Business Yorkshire New Partners
Diversity Training

Channel 4
Supporting the Channel 4 Theatre Director Scheme

Esmeé Fairbain Foundation
Regional Theatre Initiative

The PRS Foundation
Supporting the Music Creator in Residence Scheme

The theatre has the support of the Pearson Playwrights' Scheme sponsored by Pearson Plc

CHARITABLE TRUSTS

Audrey and Stanley Burton 1960 Trust

Harewood Charitable Settlement

Kenneth Hargreaves Charitable Trust

The Frances Muers Trust

Clothworkers' Foundation

The Charles Brotherton Trust

The Ragdoll Foundation

ELECTRICITY

First published in 2004 by Oberon Books Ltd.
(incorporating Absolute Classics)
521 Caledonian Road, London N7 9RH
Tel: 020 7607 3637 / Fax: 020 7607 3629

e-mail: oberon.books@btinternet.com
www.oberonbooks.com

A catalogue record for this book is available from the British
Library.

ISBN: 1 84002 437 2

Cover photo: Getty Images / Zigy Kaluzny

Printed in Great Britain by Antony Rowe Ltd, Chippenham.

Characters

JAKEY

LEO

BIZZY

KATHERINE

MICHAEL

Part I

Black.

Lights.

Dusk in an apartment on a tree-lined street in affluent North London. The end of the Summer.

The apartment is being decorated by: LEO, 46, a large man, moderate and gently spoken with traces of Welsh in his accent; JAKEY, 38, East London or Essex originally. Good looking, but past his best; BIZZY, a young 15. Mixed race. JAKEY's son. Young East London accent. Headphones permanently wrapped round his head.

The builders are dressed in white, stained overalls. The walls of the room are half-finished in sunset yellow paint. Odd, unexpected clutter lies about the room giving it the look of an archaeological dig: ornate half-finished pillars, something that might be a fountain, a plant in a pot, all barely visible beneath white protective sheets.

To the rear of the room, right of the large bay windows, a statue of the Hindu god Ganesh, completely covered. At the back left corner, an unnaturally thick exposed cable snakes out of the wall at approximately head height. Buckets, empty pots of paint, cigarette packets – the men might have bombed the building from a plane then parachuted into it themselves. Front left, a door opening inwards.

Occupying a central position, one luxurious chair, covered, upon which sits JAKEY reading the paper while LEO paints the wall stage right and BIZZY potters about to the left. A quiet, peaceful tableau disturbed, gently at first, by JAKEY.

JAKEY: (*Tutting.*) Tut tut tut tut tut.

    Continues reading.

JAKEY: Dear oh dear dear dear.

    Pause.

Can you believe it? Some people.

Pause.

Tut tut tut tut tut.

LEO: Pass me that tin of emulsion would you Bizzy?

BIZZY: This one Leo?

LEO: No no. Not the glue son. The paint. That's it.

JAKEY: Astonishing. Absolutely astonishing.

He stuffs the rest of his sandwich into his mouth.

LEO: Something in the news there Jakey?

JAKEY continues reading then turns over the page.

JAKEY: (*Without looking up.*) Some people Leo.
Honestly.

LEO prises the lid off the tin and gives the paint a stir with a stick.

LEO: Oh yes. Some people all right.

Beat.

JAKEY: This one…this prat here right, silly streak of piss,
he's got his rent money in his trousers, cash, six hundred
quid, right, it's fell out his pocket – listen Leo…who's
picked it up? His wife, right. Picked it off the floor *not
realising* it's *their* money. Doesn't twig. Thinks she just
got lucky – right.
So does she tell him? Does she 'eck. Silly moo goes out
and spends it with her girl friends. Big night out. Fancy
drinks. Throwing themselves about. Next day, her old
man's running round frantic. No rent. She realises what's
happened, tells him she spent it. He starts screaming,
calling her names.

She don't like it. Knocks him cold. One punch. Takes out his front teeth. Now he's got her in court, says he's been victimised.

He returns to the paper shaking his head.

JAKEY: '*Victimised.*' (*Beat.*)

The silly sod got married. (*Shakes head.*)

Some people.

Pause. JAKEY turns a page. LEO notes this.

LEO: You may remember there's a job of work taking place around you Jakey. (*Beat.)* Once you're done with the papers?

JAKEY reads.

LEO: Not that I'd want to intrude on your reading.

No response.

LEO: (*Gently.*) Hmm?

JAKEY: (*Still reading.*) All right Leo.

Pause.

LEO: It's just…

JAKEY flicks his paper straight.

JAKEY: Okay. All right. Call off the dogs. Dear oh dear. Here I am.

LEO regards him.

LEO: Slow and steady. That's all I ask.

JAKEY: Yeah yeah yeah. Slow and steady. Don't worry Leo. I can do that.

LEO: It's just where we're that bit behind…

LEO's attention is taken by BIZZY who has strayed towards the exposed wire, back left. He stares at it, fascinated.

LEO: (*Calmly.*) Bizzy son. Sorry to go on. Ever so nervous with you stood there.

JAKEY: (*Mildly.*) Oh for God's sake. Bizzy.

BIZZY: What?

JAKEY: Do we have to keep telling you? Keep away from the wire.

BIZZY: What?

JAKEY: It's live. Do you not understand?

BIZZY: I was nowhere near it.

JAKEY: (*Scoffing.*) *'I was nowhere near it.'*

LEO: It's dangerous son.

JAKEY: I could see how near it you were.

JAKEY takes a bite out of a new sandwich.

It's a live wire. Live!

LEO: The wire's very dangerous Bizzy.

JAKEY: He knows it's dangerous. If you touched it…

BIZZY: What?

JAKEY: *'What?'*

LEO: It could stop your heart.

JAKEY: Burnt. Inside.

LEO: You'd get heck of a shock.

BIZZY: I know.

JAKEY: Well come away then kid.

BIZZY: What about the wall?

LEO: Never mind *that* wall. Stick with this one for now. All right.

BIZZY: Yeah.

LEO: Concentrate on this one for the time being, that's it.

JAKEY: We're not short of walls Bizzy.

BIZZY: All right.

LEO: Brush? You got your brush?

BIZZY stares.

JAKEY: Fetch yer bleedin' brush. Dear oh dear.

He goes to retrieve his brush from the other side of the room.

LEO: Good lad. Good lad. There we go. Brush in hand. Good lad.

To LEO's dismay, JAKEY sits down with the paper and starts reading.

JAKEY: (*Shaking his head.*) Some people.

Pause.

LEO: All right boys. This is it. Last big push then shall we? Still a fair bit to go, so no time for slacking. Let's really get some steam up? Get this thing done, eh boys?

JAKEY: (*Immobile.*) We gotta sort that wire out Leo. Pronto.

LEO: That's all right. We will. We will.

JAKEY: Or there's gonna be an accident, you know what I mean?

LEO: We'll get it done. Don't worry about that. Mean time…

JAKEY: We should really do it now Leo.

LEO: But you know that's not possible Jakey.

JAKEY: Why not?

LEO: Because she's still working next door. She's using the computer.

JAKEY: Maybe she's finished now. Maybe she's finished, and we can turn off the electrics, mend the wire…

LEO: No no no no…

JAKEY: We could ask?

LEO: Jakey! I give you my personal guarantee. She does not wish to be disturbed, all right?

JAKEY shrugs.

LEO: We'll just keep clear of the wire, that's all. No reason it should bother us. None at all.

JAKEY: You're the boss Leo.

LEO: Precisely correct.

LEO picks up his roller hoping to lead by example.

LEO: Off we go then. Work beckons.

Beat.

JAKEY: Day after day. Never stops. Hunched up in the dark. Just her and that computer. (*He shakes his head.*) Why?

BIZZY, entranced, moves to the wire.

JAKEY: You know, with decent working conditions we would've been done by now…*Bizzy* will you come away from the wire!

BIZZY: I need the paint.

JAKEY: You got paint. What's that there ?

BIZZY: Oh right.

JAKEY looks at LEO.

JAKEY: You see!

A pause of group disappointment. JAKEY goes over to the window. A storm is gathering outside.

JAKEY: How'd we end up here Leo? Eh? In this sun-starved country. Sun-starved, that's what it is. September! That's still Summer! Every day the same filthy sky.

LEO: It was bright earlier.

JAKEY: *Bright.* You call that bright?

Beat.

What I'd give to be back in the Tropics, I tell you. Sitting outside one of them big white houses. Sipping cocktails. No worries. No sense of time.

Beat.

Local lady face down in your lap.

LEO laughs.

The two of us eh Leo! Imagine the time we'd have! And you Biz. I'd show you things!

LEO: Maybe one day.

JAKEY: *Maybe.* 'Mr. Maybe.' (*Beat.*)
Work.
That's not why we're here. That's not our purpose in life.

LEO: Hand me the ratchet would you Bizzy.

BIZZY passes LEO a hammer.

LEO: Not the hammer son. The ratchet, the ratchet.

BIZZY: Oh right.

LEO: Good lad.

Beat. LEO active.

Stay in one place. Luck knows where to find you. That's what my da' used to say.

JAKEY: Did he? Oh yeah. Found him though didn'it, eh? Luck. How old was he?

LEO: What when he passed on?

Beat.

Forty seven he was.

JAKEY: Forty seven. That's no age is it. That's barely out the blocks.

Beat.

Roofer weren't he?

LEO: No no no. (*Grandly.*) He worked on the roads..

JAKEY: The roads. Course.

LEO: Took great satisfaction from it.

JAKEY: I bet he did. The tar. The fumes. Always laughing was he?

LEO: Getting the job done right. That was his pleasure.

JAKEY: Oh yeah. Must have got a tonne of thanks 'n all. Road builder. What happened? Accident weren't it?

LEO: He was working on the Orbital, matter of fact.

Beat of sentiment.

Perfect summer's day. A few light clouds. Big orange sun set. End of the week. Cars rushing home to their families.

Beat.

A wheel. Came off a passing transit.

Back of the head it hit him. Knew nothing about it. Only spoke to my ma just ten minutes earlier.
In shock the rest of her life she was, poor love.

Beat.

JAKEY: Anyway. Bollocks. It's all a merry-go-round innit.

LEO: Oh yes Jakey.

LEO in thought.

All a merry-go-round.

JAKEY has a look around him.
Angry energy.

JAKEY: Bloody hell Leo! A six week job you told me!

Pause. LEO looks up, still distant.

I mean what the hell did she want with this place.

LEO: It's all just taken longer than expected, it's…(*Words fail.*)

JAKEY: You're not wrong there Leo! Unrealistic schedule see.

LEO: Oh, we could have coped in the time.

JAKEY: No. No see because we're missing the…we couldn't of. It's the unknown element.

LEO: …there's been the odd complication, I agree…

JAKEY: I knew it was trouble. The moment you said she wants to build a Quiet Space. What is that? Who builds a Quiet Space in a flat! I saw trouble ahead right from the off.

LEO: …but then I say to myself…if you'd just got stuck in…if…

JAKEY: Me?

LEO: Well…

JAKEY: In fairness Leo…

LEO: …no, you're right, room for improvement all round…

JAKEY: A Quiet Space. What is that?

LEO: But it's not…(complicated.)

JAKEY: It is complicated Leo.

LEO: It's just a room. A quiet room.

JAKEY: But it's…

LEO: …a quiet space. A room. What's so difficult about that?
They had them in olden times. Quite common it was. Just somewhere in the house to shut things out. Reflect on the day. A Sanctum Sanctorum.

Beat.

JAKEY: Kitchen would've been quicker.

LEO: She already has a kitchen.

JAKEY: I'm making a point.

LEO: Course when you're dealing with the unfamiliar…

JAKEY: Course, if she could've made up her mind about things.

LEO: Well in fairness Jakey…

JAKEY: In fairness Leo, she's changed her mind about everything. Black's white and white's black with her.

LEO: (*Shooshing JAKEY.*) All right all right.

Warmth from JAKEY.

JAKEY: Come on 'en. Let's get on with it shall we. No good stood around talking. What needs doing?

LEO: Right, well we still got behind the radiator; there's the ornamental fountains.

JAKEY: Wait, what? Behind the radiator?

LEO: …yes..

JAKEY: ..but if we're gonna be done by the weekend…

LEO: We get it done by/ working properly…

JAKEY: /Fine, fine!

LEO: Not by/

JAKEY: Leo, really. Fine. Fine.

LEO: /neglecting the details.

JAKEY: It's fine. Honestly.

LEO: I'm not being picky Jakey…

JAKEY: So I gotta bleed it. Get the water off.

LEO: Yes.

JAKEY: Fine. Come on then. Bizzy!

LEO: Bizzy.

JAKEY: He can't hear you. He's got his music on.

What you want him to do? Bizzy!

LEO: Bizzy!

JAKEY: He can't hear you. (*Loud.*) Bizzy! (*Soft.*) He can't hear you.

LEO: Bizzy!

JAKEY: Oy buggerlugs! He can't hear you.

JAKEY walks up to BIZZY and pulls the headphones from one ear.

JAKEY: (*Very loud.*) Oyyyy!!!

BIZZY: Aagghhh!!!

JAKEY falls about laughing.

Bastard.

JAKEY: Heh! Don't swear at your dad.

BIZZY pushes JAKEY towards the electricity source. JAKEY is off balance and gets close to the wire before he recovers himself.

JAKEY: Oy! Watch out. Bizzy! That's the live wire there.

LEO: Bizzy! Bizzy stop it now! You're pushing him into the wire. Bizzy!

JAKEY gives BIZZY a slap round the face. BIZZY stunned and quiet.

JAKEY: What you doing?

BIZZY: You scared me.

JAKEY: What the fuck?

BIZZY: I was painting.

JAKEY: Unbelievable…!

BIZZY: I was…

JAKEY: After I'd told you about the dangers.

BIZZY: I weren't thinking.

LEO: He was frightened.

JAKEY: Your own dad!

BIZZY: I didn't know. I didn't.

LEO: Do you understand how dangerous that wire is Bizzy?

BIZZY: Yes.

JAKEY raises his hand. BIZZY cowers.

JAKEY: What'm I gonna do with you?

BIZZY: I got a bad ear.

LEO: He got a shock Jakey.

JAKEY: Yeah, I'd've got a bloody shock.

LEO: He didn't mean anything.

BIZZY and LEO stare at JAKEY.

JAKEY: You don't swear at me! Understand!

BIZZY: Yeah.

JAKEY: All right. No damage done. You're all right. (*Beat.*)
    You're all right Bizzy.

BIZZY: I was frightened.

JAKEY pulls him into an embrace.

JAKEY: It's not your fault. It's her in there. Bloody lunatic.

LEO: I'm gonna sort this out.

JAKEY: You gonna speak to her?

LEO: No.

*LEO takes a few pots of paint and starts arranging them in
a semi-circle around the live wire.*

JAKEY: What you doing Leo?

LEO: You'll see in a minute.

JAKEY: Leo, what you doing?

LEO: I'm just doing this. It'll help us get along safely.

JAKEY: What you doing Leo?

LEO: See that? That's now the danger zone. No one goes inside the circle. Clear enough?

JAKEY doesn't answer.

Bizzy?

JAKEY: What you doing that for?

LEO: It's just temporary. Till we sort it out. If no one goes into it. No one'll get hurt.

JAKEY: Leo?

LEO: Yes Jakey?

JAKEY: Wouldn't it be better just to fix the fucking cable 'stead of marking out a fucking danger zone.

LEO: (*Softly.*) We can't fix the cable because she's in there working on her computer.

JAKEY: Yes but couldn't we...!

LEO: (*Loud.*) I said we can't fix the cable cause the silly moo's on her ruddy computer!

Enter KATHERINE, 32. Middle class London. Strangely abstracted having passed beyond anger. She is holding a teapot in front of her like a religious charm. She enters and says nothing for a moment.

LEO: Oh hello sweetheart.

Pause.

KATHERINE: (*Quietly, seriously, the one syllable stated like the answer to a difficult decision.*) Moo.

Pause.

LEO: Is that for us?

KATHERINE: Yes. (*Beat.*) It is.

LEO: Oh lovely. Lovely. Much obliged to you my darling. I was just thinking I could do with a fresh cup. Nice fresh cup of tea. Much obliged. Thanks everso.

Pause. Tea is not served.

Just getting onto the radiator now. We'll have to get the water off for a few minutes if that's all right.

Pause.

Lucky we got the tea in first.

KATHERINE: I thought you'd done it.

LEO: No no no. We done the radiator proper, but we haven't done behind yet.

KATHERINE: I thought you did the radiator.

Pause.

LEO: Yes. We've done the radiator proper sweetheart but...

KATHERINE: ...hours ago. I thought you did the radiator hours ago.

LEO: No no. Just this morning.

KATHERINE: Oh. Forgive me...I was under the impression that...that the morning ended at...emm...at midday. My mistake. Forgive me.

Beat.

LEO: We were just getting on to it my love. What held us back was going over where the cracks came up...back... up. Giving it a fresh coat.

KATHERINE: I need a bath.

Pause.

LEO: Oh. (*Beat.*) Well that's all right. We shan't be long. If we bleed the radiator, get the water off…

KATHERINE: I can't have a bath without water.

LEO: (*Laughing.*) No. I appreciate that. No. No. Course you can't my darling.

Pause.

Would you like us to wait till you're out…the bath…or in…it.

Pause.

KATHERINE: In it.

Pause.

LEO: Fine.

Pause.

It's coming on isn't it.

KATHERINE: Yes.

LEO: Slowly.

KATHERINE: Yes.

LEO: Well then. Nearly there now. Won't be much longer.

KATHERINE: (*Poker faced.*) And so the years march on.

Beat.

LEO: It's a lovely colour you've chosen there. Sunset yellow. It's a lovely bright warm radiant colour. Glad you didn't go with the green in the end.

Pause.

So should we bleed the radiator…or…?

Pause.

KATHERINE: What's that?

LEO: What?

KATHERINE: That there.

LEO: Oh. That's…well I had to mark out a danger zone…so we wouldn't stray into it.

KATHERINE: A danger zone?

LEO: Round the power flex. As a precaution.

KATHERINE: Could you not avoid the power flex without marking out a danger zone?

LEO: We could, but the boys were larking about a bit see, and it just seemed a touch dangerous to tell the truth.

KATHERINE: So you had to mark out a danger zone because the boys were larking about a bit.

LEO: (*Genially.*) Yes. (*Beat.*) You know…men. Boys.

Pause.

KATHERINE: What's that? Is that a crack?

LEO: Where?

KATHERINE: There running down the wall. All the way from the top to the bottom?

LEO: Oh Christ. I don't believe it. Dear dear dear dear dear dear dear.

Pause.

KATHERINE: What?

LEO: It's gone again. I'll have to redo it. Sorry lover.

KATHERINE: It keeps on cracking.

LEO: It's the subsidence see.

KATHERINE: I had the subsidence looked at.

LEO: I know. I know.

KATHERINE: I thought I'd cracked the subsidence.

LEO: I'll give it another coat tomorrow. Don't worry about anything. I'll clear it up.

KATHERINE: A new coat.

LEO: Yes.

KATHERINE: New coat for Christmas.

Pause.

LEO: See it looks to me you've still got that problem. I don't know.

Pause. LEO's gaze wanders to the window.

Look at that beautiful tree. Lovely street this. Lovely road. Beautiful tree. What a shame it's been such a nuisance to you.

Pause.

Don't worry sweetheart. We'll put it right.

KATHERINE: Yes.

LEO: Of course we will. You'll have your Quiet Space very soon, I give you my word. All quiet. All lovely.

Pause.

Was there something else.
(*Beat.*) You wanted to say?

KATHERINE: Yes there was.

She turns on her heels and exits, with tea.
Pause: LEO exhales. JAKEY sits himself down and picks up the paper, shaking his head as if some great truth had just been confirmed to him.

LEO: Damn it.

LEO puts his head in his hand.

LEO: I do it every time.

JAKEY: Do what Leo?

LEO: The minute I start speaking to her it's all 'sweetheart' and 'lover' and Christ knows what. I know I'm doing it but I can't help myself.
It's nerves you see.
I feel nervous and I drivel on like an halfwit.

JAKEY reads, unconcerned.

JAKEY: Moo.

LEO: (*Head in hands.*) Oh God!

JAKEY: Don't take it personal Leo.

LEO: How can I not?

Pause.

LEO: See, all this talk. There's not been enough progress.

BIZZY: Why's she angry with us?

JAKEY: The progress is fine.

LEO: You been eating and talking.

JAKEY: Is that wrong?

LEO: She wants to see progress.

JAKEY: She's got progress.

LEO: Eating and talking. Eating and talking.

JAKEY: Is that wrong Leo?

LEO: She wants to see changes!

Pause.

JAKEY: Changes? Leo. Look. (*Arms out.*) Will you look!

Beat.

Yellow. *Yellow.* Everything yellow.
Look.

He stands like a circus ring-leader uncovering the sheets to show half-finished waterfalls.

Look! Waterfalls. Indoors. Look Leo!
Look! (*He whips the sheet of the Ganesh statue.*)
Babah the fucking elephant.

LEO: Ganesh.

JAKEY: Elephants. Waterfalls. Yellow. Leo! This room has gone through *the change.*

LEO: (*Clapping hands.*) Come on. Right now! Radiator.

JAKEY: See, maybe you shouldn't've said we'd not *done* the radiator.

LEO: She could see we hadn't done it Jakey.

JAKEY gives LEO's back a little massage.

JAKEY: All right Leo. Don't get all tense. (*Beat.*) So she can see through solids can she?

LEO tenses up.

LEO: Look, she…

JAKEY: Shhh. It's all right.

Beat.

You should have just put on everything was going to plan.

LEO wrenches free of JAKEY's healing hands.

LEO: (*Raising his voice.*) In view of the fact we've been here seventeen weeks longer than…

JAKEY: Just don't admit your errors.

LEO: It's not about admitting…(your errors)!

JAKEY: What's time to a woman anyway?

LEO: It's not about time…or…or…women…

JAKEY: See if we hadn't been talking non-stop.

LEO: In all fairness Jakey…

JAKEY: In all fairness Leo, if we'd applied ourselves…

LEO: Jakey, in all fairness…

JAKEY: …in all fairness Leo, mind you don't go into the danger zone…

LEO checks his position.

LEO: I'm nowhere near the danger zone.

JAKEY grabs LEO and pushes him.

JAKEY: Ha ha ha. Really? Ha ha ha

They wrestle.

LEO: Ow. Ow. Jakey! Watch out! The wire! Jakey the wire!

Wrestling. Then it subsides.

That wasn't funny.

JAKEY: Sorry Leo.

LEO: Stop pissing about now. Okay! I've had enough!

JAKEY: I'm really sorry.

Pause. LEO seizes JAKEY.

LEO: You will be in a minute.

They wrestle.

JAKEY: Ahghh. Ahghh. Leo! Watch out!

LEO: Ha ha ha ha.

LEO is stronger than JAKEY who begins to panic.

JAKEY: Leo!

BIZZY: Ha ha ha ha.

JAKEY: Leo! Get off me! Leo!!

LEO lets him go. He's not fit and the exertion takes its toll.

JAKEY: Fucking hell man. I was almost touching the wire.

LEO: So was I!

JAKEY: It was right near my neck!

LEO laughs and wheezes. Can't catch his breath.

JAKEY: You all right?

LEO: I'm fine. Fine.

JAKEY: He' y' are. Have some water. Sit down.

LEO: I'm all right.

But he sits down anyway.

JAKEY: You haven't been doing your sit-ups Leo.

LEO: No.

JAKEY: Look at you.

LEO: I'm fine! Come on. Enough horsing around.
Let's get on with it.

JAKEY: Fine.

LEO: Good.

Pause. Sitting a moment longer.

JAKEY: I tell you something.
When I had the business, I was stressing out over stupid

things. Screaming at people for no reason and that.
Getting violent. Hitting Bizzy. Maiming friends.
It's no good.

Pause.

I looked at them underneath me. The company's going
down the pan. They couldn't give a toss.
You know, the British worker and all that…rah rah rah,
but my fucking workers couldn't give a monkey's.
They had a smoke, they had a natter. They weren't in
any hurry. I thought, what do I want with this. I could be
down there. Take my orders. Carry out my tasks. Take it
a bit easier. Know what I mean?
(*Beat.*) So I'm not going to tear myself up cause some
stuck-up miss can't live without her fucking *Quiet Space*
for another few days, you know what I'm saying?

Enter KATHERINE to men sitting. Pause.

LEO: Hello love.

Pause.

Come on now boys. Let's get on shall we.

Pause.

Just getting that radiator off now my love. Come on
then Jakey, give us an hand.

BIZZY: We have to bleed it first.

LEO: Oh yes of course. We haven't bled it yet.

Pause.

Everything all right my love?

KATHERINE: Yes.

LEO: Good good.

Pause.

KATHERINE: I'm not…um…I don't know anything about…I mean…I don't know who your love is…but…um…it isn't me.

Pause.

LEO: What's that? Oh God. I'm sorry sweetheart I'm sorry. It's just…

KATHERINE: I don't…

LEO: No. No. Fair enough. Point taken.

KATHERINE: I don't usually mind, but you do it so often.

LEO: Do I? I didn't realise darling. That's fine.

KATHERINE: Oh God I'm sorry.

LEO: That's all right darling. You don't have to…

KATHERINE: No. No. No. No.

LEO: Really sweetheart. You don't have to…

KATHERINE: I know! I know I don't have to apologise!

Pause.

Why am I apologising? That's me. Always apologising. And then afterwards I'm angry. I should have written this down. Dammit I should have written this down. It's been going round my head for days.
I've prepared a speech.
While I was working, I found myself preparing a speech. Something I would say to you all, and now I wish I'd written it down. Oh well. That's not what life's about is it. Speeches. Sorry…you look confused. Forgive my formality…but…but…there is no other way for me. You see.

Pause.

Well look. Let me begin by saying, you're not to take this personally.

You're all good men I'm sure but I decided not to flirt with you. I have my reasons. I've not been feeling very physical, that's the truth. I've felt very disconnected from my body, so I couldn't play with you.

I thought instead I'd try and earn your respect. But I've failed.

Like I said. You're not to take this personally.

If I say something along the lines of…I regard you as pigs…, don't take it personally. It's not personal. I don't really know you, so how can it be. I've tried to reach out, make contact, but we haven't…we haven't been able to cement this relationship. Ha ha.

You're happy enough with your own company…you don't want me to intrude – which is fine, except this is of course my front room. I mean, this is the largest room in the flat you've occupied for the past three months. So if sometimes what I say sounds personal, I apologise. Off I go again. Apologising. Could you teach me not to, do you think? I mean, you've shared my space here, you've helped yourself to my food, you've expressed yourselves very loudly and boldly – we'll come to that later – you've been reading my diary. At least, somebody has, because I know. Important messages have been erased from the answerphone. A set of my keys has vanished. You've stodged up my toilet countless times so that I never…never quite know what I'll find when I go into it, and yet I hear you, every day, singing and shouting and laughing uproariously as if this were some sort of drinking club.

Expressing opinions. Opinions. Opinions.

Without apology.

I'm sorry. I wasn't eavesdropping. But the walls are thin. You must know.

You've had your hands inside them.

I've plugged up my ears, but your voices have a way of carrying through. Me…I…I have to struggle to be heard. Not in any crusading sort of a way. I mean literally. I often can't be heard. Because I won't raise my voice above a certain level. But you…everything you've said since you began your stay has…penetrated…me.

So I'm sorry again for overhearing your conversation, but I struggled against it, I really did.

Words words.

Food. Food.

My food began to disappear. One day. Okay. As you never tire of saying, I can afford it. It's only a biscuit. But as a matter of fact, it wasn't just a biscuit. A leg of chicken went. A side of ham. A few bars of chocolate. A bottle of wine. You're right. I can afford it. Of course I can. And no, I'm not starving, of course not. But when I have food in the house, I expect it to be there when I want it.

What if I had guests and nothing to serve them. Oh I know it seems unlikely now, but there were guests – once upon a time. Do you see my point?

So I thought to myself, 'does that make me wicked? Should I not buy a little extra, if I know it'll go.' Which is what I did. But you're professionals. You're not the starving of Africa. And anyway, when I asked…did someone take my chocolate…you said nothing in reply. And it seemed to me, a) that's not a very manly thing to do. To go quiet. And secondly…b) why was I thinking of you whilst I was shopping? Why was I thinking of what to buy you when you can't even manage a hello in the mornings.

It's my own fault. I wanted to be independent. I didn't take advice. I've shut people out who wanted to help me. I've shut people out.

Perhaps I should have fired you once I knew how inefficient you were. And yet…I kept thinking, give them a chance. They can't be that bad, and anyway, who's to say I wouldn't have the same trouble all over again? So in the end…I kept you on.

So here we are and…(*Indicating white sheets.*)…well, I don't really know what's under all that. I don't know if you're half way through or nearly done or…doubling back from the brink of completion to…the chaos of birth ha ha ha.

The men's faces show incomprehension.

Time.

Time.

Perhaps if I felt more myself, none of this would have happened. Perhaps if I'd felt my body was my own, I could have teased more work out of you, but instead…

…instead you…you…I'm trying not to exaggerate…you strip me of my dignity…and…I'm trying to steer clear of this word, because it's so loaded. So forceful…and yet…yes, it does feel like a sort of *rape.* Yes. And it's really come home to me that being a human being, one has needs beyond…beyond the bodily…beyond a roof over one's head, the need to subsist…and…

(*She laughs.*) I'm so sorry. I've lost you. Wouldn't it be better if I just *judged and condemned.* Isn't that what most people do? Isn't that what *you* do? I wonder do you ever experience this…this feeling that you're so utterly divorced…when I say divorced, I don't mean unique…I don't mean superior…but do you ever feel…plainly put…that you have no *right* to speak…ha? Do you? Ha ha ha. Probably not…that certain very simple things are much easier for other people…sorry. I'm trying to be specific, but I know I sound like a terrible old…oh god, you must think I'm a witch.

What I'm trying to say is…you might say…oh, so-and-so's a 'tosser.' Or 'I hate the French,' that's right. I heard that. For French, substitute any race on earth. It doesn't matter. I've heard it all. And, I thought to myself, 'how's it possible to say something so bold.' I hate the French.

We're all the same aren't we? We all need the same things. No. There's the…is it class? is it a class thing I wonder. I've lost you again. (*Laughing.*) I'm sorry. Look at you. You think I'm nuts don't you.

How you finding the work? (*Laughs.*) This one's quiet isn't he. What? (*She puts her hands to her chest. Looks down.*) They're just breasts? (*She indicates her face.*) Here. This is me. I'm here.

Pause.

Well. I won't apologise. Just finish the work. You will finish soon won't you? Because I just…I just…(*Laughs.*) I don't want you in my flat any more. I'd like to carry on life without you. If that's okay.

Sudden shift to serious.

Right.

She inhales deeply as if in grief.

It's all right. If I cry, it doesn't mean there's a problem

Pause.

There's nothing wrong with me. (*Beat.*) I'm fine. I'm not one of those girls that's forever crying.

(*Pause.*) Just sometimes…when I let out emotion. That's all.

(*Pause.*) And sometimes I cry because…because the more I speak, the less I communicate. And sometimes talking's the thing that gets in the way. God. Back to cliches.

'*Talking's the thing that gets in the way.*'

(*She looks out the window.*) That tree…that beautiful, beautiful tree speaks more powerfully to me than any word or opinion yet uttered by man upon this earth.

Pause.

Well look, I feel a lot better. I feel you know me now. I think we can move on from here.

Beat. LEO tries to find words.

You don't have to say anything.

LEO gives up.

Right.

Exit. Door bangs off. Prolonged silence, each man with his own thoughts, careful that eyes don't meet.

LEO: Would you bleed the radiator please Jakey.

JAKEY: Course I would Leo.

BIZZY: Should I help him Leo?

LEO: Please Bizzy.

BIZZY: Right you are.

Pause.

JAKEY: Other side son.

BIZZY: Right.

A long jet of water into a bucket.

JAKEY: Slow and steady.

Pause.

Here she comes.

Beat.

Caw. There's a lot in her.

Water over the floor.

Bucket under the water son. Going over the floor boards.

Water in bucket.

Good lad.

Bucket filling.

Up to much tonight Leo?

LEO: Not much Jakey no.

JAKEY: Not going to the pub for one.

LEO: Don't think so tonight Jakey no.

JAKEY: Right.

Water stops.

That should do her.
So. What's the plan. Do behind the radiator…then what?

Pause.

LEO: Did she leave the building?

JAKEY: Think so Leo.

LEO: She's not been out before.

JAKEY: Not with us here.

Beat.

LEO: Worries me that.

JAKEY: Shouldn't let it worry you Leo.

Beat.

JAKEY: She never had her bath.

LEO: No. She never did.

Pause.

JAKEY: P'raps she's coming back for it.

Beat.

LEO: Perhaps Jakey, yes.

JAKEY: Oh well.

Pause.

You know what I find though. You can know a woman your whole life, then one day she turns round says she's gone off you.

Beat.

Suddenly you're just the last person she fucked, and you mean even less than a total stranger.
Do you know what I mean Leo?

LEO: Would you mind getting the water off Bizzy.

BIZZY: All right.

JAKEY: That's why I don't get involved any more.

LEO: You know which one it is don't you?

BIZZY: Yeah.

LEO: You sure now?

BIZZY: Yeah.

LEO: The tap behind the boiler.

BIZZY: Yeah, I know.

LEO: Off you go then.

Exit BIZZY. LEO waits for him to go and then...

LEO: Has Bizzy been stealing her food?

JAKEY: What?

LEO: Has Bizzy been stealing her food?

JAKEY: Leo!

LEO: Did he eat her chicken?

JAKEY: Silly question. 'Did he eat her chicken.'

LEO: (*Snapping.*) Did he or not? Answer me.

JAKEY: He may of. I don't know.

LEO: (*Purposeful.*) Right.

LEO starts packing BIZZY's hold-all.

JAKEY: Leo!?

LEO: I'm sorry Jakey. I wanted to give him a chance. I wanted to bring him into the fold.

JAKEY: Leo. You can't! What, because of her?

LEO: Did he read her diary?

JAKEY: I don't know. (*Beat.*) What if he did? What would it mean to him anyway?

LEO: I thought he was supposed to have a photographic memory!

JAKEY: He does, but…(*Tapping his head.*)…it's a shit camera he's got Leo..

LEO: Oh very nice. Very nice thing to do to a person that. Reading her diary.

JAKEY: You're over-reacting!

LEO: Oh! Over-reacting is it? Over-reacting!

JAKEY: That's Bizzy! It's not his fault. That's just how he is.

LEO: Well then.

JAKEY: He can't help it.

LEO: He's not my responsibility.

JAKEY: But he's mine Leo. He's *my* responsibility. What can I do?

Enter BIZZY.

BIZZY: Is it the red one or the blue one?

LEO: The blue one son, the blue one.

BIZZY: I did the red one.

JAKEY: Turn the red one back on and do the blue one.

BIZZY: All right Leo.

Exit BIZZY.

JAKEY: He still needs looking after.

LEO: (*Decisively.*) Then why don't you both go together! (*JAKEY stares.*) Yes. Why not! Both of you!

JAKEY: Hang on.

LEO: I could call the job centre right now have 'em send me a pair of ruddy remedials more up to it than the pair of you!

JAKEY: (*Genuinely taken aback.*) Leo!

LEO: I'm sorry Jakey, but I've never…

JAKEY: Excuse me, but have you forgotten?

LEO: No – but I've never in my life been/ spoken to like that…

JAKEY: You seem to have forgotten?

LEO: Never. Not by anyone in all my working life…

JAKEY: Have you/forgotten…

LEO: Oh, if I paid you to eat and smoke, then you'd earn your money, then you'd be fine/ if that's what the wage was for…?

JAKEY: /Have you forgotten Leo? I'm asking/ have you forgotten?

LEO: (*Shouting*.) /Yes, I am grateful for the help you gave me Jakey…

JAKEY: Grateful.

LEO: But it doesn't give you the right to bury my business. It doesn't give you the right.

JAKEY: The money I gave you…

LEO: I'm grateful for the money, but that was…

JAKEY: …coming to me cap in hand…old uncompromising Leo…

LEO:…of course, I'm boundlessly grateful for the…

JAKEY: Boundlessly…

LEO: For the money Jakey. (*Shouting*.) I just want to get this ruddy Quiet Space completed is all for pity's sake! (*Beat – then quiet*.) I just want to get this done.

Subdued pause.

JAKEY: It's one of those jobs. You get 'em. Be over soon. She'll be happy.

LEO: 'She'll be happy.'

JAKEY: She will Leo. We'll finish it off really nice. She'll be all smiles, I promise. A Quiet Space. We'll put it right. We'll give that woman a room so fucking tranquil, she'll jump when she farts.

Pause.

All right Leo?

LEO looks up with defeat in his eyes.

JAKEY: We've turned the corner.

Pause: sober.

LEO: Just understand. This is my living. My living. It's not a game. And it's precarious. Every year I've had to work harder to get by.

JAKEY: (*Intent.*) You're telling that to *me*!? To *me* Leo. Think about it With what I've been through!

LEO: Of course I'm grateful for the help you…

JAKEY: No. Nothing. It's fine,

LEO: …you gave me the start I needed…that money…without it…

JAKEY: Really. Fine. Nothing. Nothing.

LEO: …it's been a tough old slog for me.

JAKEY: Leo!

Beat.

You're a very committed worker. (*Smile.*)

Pause – laughter.

LEO: You little piss-taker.

JAKEY: I'm not.

LEO: You bloody monkey.

JAKEY: Leo?

LEO looks.

JAKEY: I understand.

LEO scans JAKEY's face for the truth and then nods.

JAKEY: I understand.

Pause. BIZZY enters, smiling hugely, with three large glasses of Ribena on a tray.

BIZZY: I got you Ribena.

LEO and JAKEY exchange disappointed looks.

(*Pause.*) What?

LEO: From now on, we don't take from the kitchen. Got it?

BIZZY: It's just Ribena.

JAKEY: Go and pour it back.

BIZZY: But I…

JAKEY: Go and pour it back Bizzy!

BIZZY: You can't pour…it's mixed…

JAKEY: (*Angrily.*) Put it back coz we don't take from the fridge no more.

BIZZY: It weren't in the fridge.

JAKEY: We don't take anything!

BIZZY: All right.

LEO: He's all right. You're all right Bizzy. You get the water off?

BIZZY: (*Moodily.*) Yeah.

LEO: You wanna go and check?

JAKEY: Yeah.

LEO: We're all going to make a special effort from now on all right son?

BIZZY: Yeah.

JAKEY: Just these last few days. Or you won't be able to come and help us no more. All right?

BIZZY: Yeah.

JAKEY: I'll have to put you back in special school.

BIZZY: I don't like special school.

JAKEY: I know you don't Biz.

BIZZY: I don't wanna go there.

JAKEY: But we won't have no choice will we. If you can't make yourself useful.

BIZZY: I thought I was useful.

LEO: Leave it Jakey. You're all right Bizzy. Let's have that radiator off and get out of here.

JAKEY: What about the electrics?

LEO: We'll do the electrics tomorrow.

JAKEY: But…

LEO: No. Not without her say-so. She'll have something running and…no way.

JAKEY: Fine.

LEO: But tomorrow, we really get some steam up. All right.

JAKEY: Yeah.

LEO: No excuses. No mucking about.

JAKEY: Fine.

LEO: We bring our own tea in flasks.

JAKEY: Leo?

LEO: Understood?!

JAKEY: Of course.

LEO: From now on, we strive for perfection in every
    smallest detail. Bizzy? Jakey?

JAKEY: We won't let you down Leo.

LEO stares hard.

LEO: You'd better bloody not, or that's it. We're finished.

Black.

Dramatic music. A storm.

Night becomes day. A note of mystery.

Cocks crow.

Part II

Early the next morning and the sun is breaking through after the storm. At lights up, BIZZY is bent over a Black and Decker work bench. JAKEY is reading a paper and smoking a Marlboro Red. A Sunday, day-of-rest sort of feeling.

JAKEY: Dear oh dear dear dear dear dear.

Pause.

Without his eyes leaving the paper, he reaches into his bag and removes a gigantic sandwich. He takes a bite.

Gawd. Some people.

The work bench collapses. JAKEY turns and stares: BIZZY puzzles: he has the bench upside down and can't figure it out. He takes an age trying to put it up. JAKEY watches, chewing, shaking his head every now and then.

JAKEY: What you doing?

BIZZY: What?

JAKEY: What are you doing?

BIZZY: I'm doing the Black and Dee.

JAKEY: What you doing to it?

BIZZY gestures as if explanation were unneccesary. He gestures again before he finds words. Repeat x 3.

BIZZY: Putting it up.

JAKEY: But it's upside down.

BIZZY stares hard, then figures it out and all is suddenly clear.

Simple innit.

BIZZY: Yeah.

JAKEY shakes his head.

JAKEY: Dear oh dear…

He returns to his paper and doesn't look up.

How'd we get in this game eh? (*Shakes head. Turns the page.*) I mean me working for Leo. Plodding Leo! 'S all back to front.

Beat. Puts down his paper.
When I had the business Bizzy. Richest man on the street I was.
Wanted for nothing. Car. Holidays.
Latest appliances.

BIZZY: Where'd it all go?

JAKEY: Well you ain't cheap for starters!

BIZZY: Oh right.

JAKEY: Naaahh. The banks. That's who it was.
That prize Berkley Hunt in the bank.

Beat.
Knifed me he did. (*Beat.*) Knifed the business. Finished it.

Beat.
Some people.

Beat.
You know what I'd do? If he walked in now, you know what I'd do?

BIZZY: No.

JAKEY: I'd lie him on the floor and push that live bloody wire right up his Khyber Passage.

BIZZY: Would you?

JAKEY: Love to.

BIZZY stares.

BIZZY: Wouldn't that burn his heart and liver out and stuff?

JAKEY stares at his son uncomprehendingly, then shakes his head.

JAKEY: You wanna roll? I made you a roll.

BIZZY: What is it?

JAKEY gets a clingfilm wrapped roll out the bag.

JAKEY: Egg. You like egg.

BIZZY: I only like egg with cucumber.

JAKEY: It's got cucumber.

BIZZY opens it up doubtfully and checks inside.

It's got cucumber!

BIZZY starts eating. JAKEY shakes his head and laughs. The two of them eating sandwiches as if they'd gone fishing.

JAKEY: 'Burn his heart out.' What are you like?

Laughs more, with BIZZY.

Bloody would as well. Little bloody tyrant stuck behind his desk making decisions. Right up his Khyber I would. See how he liked that.

BIZZY laughs.

Would've flourished. My business. Course it would. Good little business it was. (*Beat.*) Pen-pushing bloody rat. 'The debt must be repaid. We can't do any more for you.'

BIZZY: Pen-pushing bloody rat.

JAKEY: Too right. (*Chews.*) Billions they got Bizzy. These banks. Billions. But it's my money they want back. Nevermind the loss of livelihoods.

He checks his watch.

Wonder where Leo is.

BIZZY: Don't know.

JAKEY: Funny him being late. After yesterday. (*He starts giggling.*) Caw dear oh dear…his face when she was going off.

BIZZY laughs with him.

BIZZY: Oh no…

Another thought renders him incapapble of speech for laughter.

JAKEY: Oh God.

BIZZY: What?

JAKEY: M…(*Laughter.*)…M…(*Terrible laughter…then…*) Moo.

BIZZY laughs.

BIZZY: Moo.

JAKEY: Moo.

JAKEY wipes a tear, sobering.

(*Beat.*) Poor old Leo. (*Beat.*) Plodding away. (*Beat.*) Plodding Leo. (*Beat.*)
(*Beat.*) See he never remarried when his old dear passed on.(*Beat.*) Couldn't put it behind him.
(*Beat.*) Great big boiler she was.(Beat.) Nothing wrong with that. (*Beat.*) You don't want one them skinny ones Bizzy. No way. (*Beat.*) But Leo's missis. (*Beat.*) Caw dear oh dear. (*Beat.*)
Fell out an ugly tree she did. (*Beat.*) Hit every branch the way down.(*Beat.*) Shocking looking girl.

Beat.

See you gotta get the roll of the dice in this bloody carnival son. (*He regards BIZZY somewhat sadly.*) And some people, they don't get the luck.

Shakes his head.

See with Leo's missis, they couldn't do nothing about it. (*Beat.*) Every night the year he'd be down that hospital. Rain or shine.(Beat.) Devoted he was. (*Beat.*) No kids. (*Beat.*) Just Leo now. That's where it ends. Gentle plodding Leo shall be the last.

Pause – JAKEY up and about.

I ever tell you about them two black girls I had?

BIZZY: Which ones?

JAKEY: Oh, it were going back a few year. When I still had the business. Back when I still had the Audi. Nice girls. Church goers. They've come back to mine, and one of them's off in the loo, the other one's come in. Beautiful. High heels. Legs. I was quite charming in them days. She comes in, doesn't say a word, pulls at her little mini, it's come off like a sweet wrapper. Must have been velcro or something.

BIZZY: Velcro?

JAKEY: That's it. So there I am, three in the afternoon, staring into her Quiet Space, gazing into the heart of Africa, in walks her friend...

Enter LEO. Pale, feverish. Short-winded. Pause.

Leo.

LEO: Sorry boys.

JAKEY: Where've you been?

LEO: Really. So sorry.

He lays down his bag and bends over for breath.

JAKEY: Christ, you look terrible.

LEO: Didn't sleep.

JAKEY: You all right?

LEO: Oh fine-not-a-bother, fine-not-a-bother.

JAKEY: (*Doubtfully.*) Well I'm pleased to hear you are.

LEO still short of breath.

LEO: Okay. All right. New day. New day. Shall we get cracking then eh?

JAKEY stares at BIZZY.

JAKEY: What's he like Biz?

LEO: I mean it. Come on boys.

JAKEY: Well, yeah, but hang on. We gotta finish our breakfast first.

LEO: (*Impatient.*) We have to get started. We have to make a dent.

JAKEY: Eh! Eh! Roll back. Roll back a minute Leo. Look. Behind the radiator. (*LEO looks doubtful.*) Go on! Have a look.

LEO does so.

LEO: You did it.

JAKEY: While you was curled up in bed. So now we're having our breakfast ta very much..

LEO: Sorry. So sorry lads. I've had…it's been an hectic sort of a night.

JAKEY: What's the matter with you?

He shakes his head in confusion.

LEO: Don't know. Don't know. Must be coming down with something. Chokin' in bed I was…had the fear I did. Don't know where it came in from. Every time I shut my eyes to sleep, I was back in this room…

JAKEY: Puff! It's happened again. Ha ha ha.

LEO: …only…(*He moves to the window.*)…the tree outside…it was listening.

LEO: I went to close the curtains, but it thrust out an arm…a branch…through the window and turned like a corkscrew up through my boots. Twisting, twisting, twisting, up through my legs, like woody veins, sucking out the last drops of moisture in my body…

JAKEY: (*Laughing.*) …which brings us back to them two black girls I had…

LEO: I looked up, and in the tree, there was a face. An old old face. Of a woman. She started to speak. 'You've defiled holy ground' she said. 'You've defiled holy ground.'

JAKEY shakes his head. But LEO is really out of sorts, sweating.

JAKEY: You chapel-goers. What are you like eh?

LEO: Is it very cold in here?

JAKEY: It's warm Leo.

LEO: I must be coming down with something. Ah well.

JAKEY: Take it easy all right.

LEO: Not today. We can't take it easy today Jakey, you promised me.

BIZZY's gravitated to the wire again.

LEO: Oh sweet Jesus, he's…

JAKEY intervenes.

JAKEY: Bizzy son.

He turns.

JAKEY: Not in the danger zone.

BIZZY: I thought that was the danger zone.

JAKEY: No no. The bit round the wire's …(*To LEO.*) He just
wants attention, that's all.

LEO: Attention is it?

JAKEY: Like living in a bloody loop with Bizzy.

LEO: Shall we fix it now then?

JAKEY: Well…I don't know about that.

LEO: Where is she? Is she in her room?

JAKEY: No.

Shudder of fear.

LEO: Where then?

JAKEY: I don't know.

LEO: What do you mean you don't know?

JAKEY: Do I know where she goes?

LEO: She goes nowhere! She sits in her room!

JAKEY: Well she's not there now.

LEO: So where is she?

JAKEY: I said 'I don't know.'

LEO: So who let you in?

JAKEY: The door was open.

LEO: The door was open?

JAKEY: (*Emphasising the normality.*) Yeah.

LEO: But…

JAKEY: The door was open, we just came in…

LEO: But this is unheard of…this is…

JAKEY: I know…I know, but Leo…

LEO: After yesterday…it worries me Jakey…I don't like it…

JAKEY: Leo. Relax would you!

LEO: Yes but…alone in her flat…why would she…

JAKEY: (*Smiling.*) We're not alone Leo. That's what I'm trying to say. There's someone else.

LEO looks incredulous – like caught in a trap.

LEO: Someone else?

JAKEY: Yes.

LEO: Where?

JAKEY: In her room.

LEO: Who?

JAKEY: I don't know. He called out.

LEO: 'He?'

JAKEY: It surprised me too.

LEO: Who is 'he'?

JAKEY: Said he'd join us in a while.

LEO: (*In a panic.*) Who is he Jakey! What the hell's going on!

JAKEY: Heh! Calm down. What's the matter with you?

LEO: What man Jakey? What man is in her room?

JAKEY: Do I know? I don't know! He asked not to be disturbed.

LEO: But we need to sort the electrics…and there's no…authority…in the flat…there's no…I'll go and speak to him.

JAKEY: I shouldn't do that.

LEO: Why not?

JAKEY: He asked not to be disturbed.

LEO: But I feel…I feel very uncomfortable Jakey…

JAKEY: He was quite clear about it…

LEO: But…I feel lost…we have no direction…

JAKEY: 'No direction.'

LEO: The…the…room…everything will spiral out…

JAKEY: You wanna cup of tea Leo?

LEO: We need to get a grounding…a…

JAKEY: Sit down. Nice soothing cup of tea?

LEO: (*Decisively.*) I'm going to speak to him.

JAKEY: But he asked…

LEO: I know, I know but we have things to do…the electrics…we have our commitments…

JAKEY: He was very clear…

LEO: Just a quick word. Then we can get some steam up.

JAKEY: I'd give it a minute or two.

LEO: No no. It's fine. Quick word should do it. Then we'll press on. Make a go of it. I'll just have a quick word with him. That'll do it.

LEO exits – JAKEY and BIZZY stare.
Off, we hear a rapping on a door…

LEO: (*Off.*) Hello?

Another rapping.

LEO: (*Off.*) Sorry to intrude.

Then off, door opening. Commotion.

MICHAEL: (*Off – angrily.*) Didn't I ask not to be disturbed? I'm occupied damn it! Don't you get it?

LEO: (*Off.*) So sorry. Was just wondering…

LEO back into the room cowering, MICHAEL just a voice, off, pursuing him.

MICHAEL: Five minutes, that's all I asked . Five minutes damn it, what's the matter with you? Don't you have ears?

LEO: Ever so sorry, just had no idea who you were…

MICHAEL: So now I have to clock in with the damned builder, is that it? For crying out loud! (*Beat.*) I'll speak to you in five minutes. Kindly don't disturb me again. Thank you so much!

He exits.
LEO looks miserably at JAKEY. JAKEY and BIZZY stare.

LEO: Anyhow…I…I drove down to Reading last night. An old pal of mine specialises in decorative wall-craft.

Beat.

Good news! I managed to get hold of some beading exactly like the beading on the wall we've made a mess of.

JAKEY: We haven't made a mess of any wall Leo?

LEO: We made a mess of the beading Jakey.

JAKEY: It hasn't been mentioned?

LEO: She mentioned it to me.

JAKEY: What she say?

LEO: (*Exploding.*) For pity's sake, can you not just accept my instructions without argument. Just once!

Beat.

Look! Do you see any beading? I don't. Why's that? Because you can't see the ruddy beading, the paint's on so ruddy thick. Look at it! It's like a ruddy blind man chucked the paint out a ruddy bucket!

JAKEY: (*Stifling a laugh.*) You can still make out the patterns.

LEO: Begin again. Give the surfaces a good scrub with the sand-paper, then get the new beading up according to this plan. Apply a thin coat of paint, do be sparing. It'll come up lovely.

JAKEY: One step forward, two steps back.

LEO: If we all muck in, should only take a half hour or so. (*Beat.*) Bizzy?

BIZZY: What?

LEO: Good lad. Remember our vows? Commitment boys! Commitment. Today we really get some steam up.

They all pick up their tools and start a sort of preliminary phase of work.

LEO: That's it. Up and at 'em. We'll have a good day today, I know we will. We'll be all right.

JAKEY: Funny us never having seen him. All this time.

LEO: Who's that?

JAKEY: The boyfriend. Assuming he is. Funny he's not shown his face.

LEO: Doesn't matter. Not important.

JAKEY: All right Leo. Just having a natter.

Pause.

So I guess they haven't done it in a month. Eh Bizzy?

LEO: Keep with the rhythms of the sanding. Very therapeutic. Calms the body. Soothing.

Beat.

JAKEY: I mean, she just had that way about her. Like…if you touched her…she'd go off…There's something about her. She's definitely got something.

LEO: Very much rather we didn't talk about her at all actually Jakey.

JAKEY: Fair enough Leo.

LEO: If it's all the same to you.

Beat.

JAKEY: Don't see it does any harm mind you.

LEO: I'd just very much rather…

JAKEY: People need a bit of love. That's what I think. Or they go off. That's the way we are. That's how it is.

LEO: (*Strongly.*) Yes, but with respect, Jakey, it's not *love* that animates this conversation. It's malicious tittle-tattle around the carnal relations of two people we know nothing whatever about!

And then, casually from the back…

BIZZY: I know about him.

JAKEY: Course you do son.

BIZZY: He works in a bank.

BIZZY continues working.

JAKEY: (*Sarcastic.*) Mmhmm?

BIZZY: They haven't done it in a month.

JAKEY: That's how it looks.

BIZZY: He asked her to marry him…

JAKEY gets interested. Stops work.

JAKEY: Who did?

BIZZY: Michael. He asked her to marry him…and she said yes but then her mum died and she said no.

LEO and JAKEY stare at each other.

JAKEY: How'd you know that Bizzy?

LEO: Oh gawd…

BIZZY: (*Helpfully.*) Her book. She said yes. She accepted first of all. But then she changed her mind and stopped him coming here. She won't see him now.

LEO: Oh Christ. Her diary. He read her blimmin' diary!

JAKEY: Oh gawd! No. Biz!

BIZZY: She said she'd marry him but then she changed her mind. (*Beat.*) Innit.

JAKEY and LEO stare at each other.

JAKEY: Bizzy! You can't!

LEO: See this…this is unspeakably…

JAKEY: Bizzy. (*Beat.*) Leo…

BIZZY: (*Helpfully.*) Her mum died. When her mum died from cancer, she couldn't sleep with him no more. She had other fantasies. Really good ones.

JAKEY: All right. Enough now Bizzy.

BIZZY: She's worried she's addicted to sex because she wants it so much. She wants it all the time. That's all she thinks about every day. She goes out at night and finds people. It's written in her book. Men. But she can't do it with Michael no more cause she's changed.

LEO: Oh my God!

JAKEY: Bizzy…Bizzy…that was her diary…you can't read her diary…don't ever…EVER say things from her diary, understand!

BIZZY: You said I had to read books cause they told you things!

JAKEY: Yeah but…(*He pulls BIZZY across the room away from LEO.*) Say nothing. *Nothing.* About the diary. All right. The diary. That's thoughts in her head right. That's different from a book, right. That's private. How would you like someone reading thoughts in your head eh?

BIZZY stares blankly.

JAKEY: All right. Don't think about it.

BIZZY: Reading thoughts in my head…

LEO: (*In desperation.*) For crying out loud!

JAKEY: It's all right Leo. He won't say nothing. Bizzy! You don't say none of that, you hear ?

BIZZY: None of what?

JAKEY: Exactly! (*Turns to LEO.*) He can't help it. He's got a photographic memory. It's not his choice. It goes in and sticks. It's there. It's on film. It doesn't matter.

LEO: Why! Why! Why'd he have to read her ruddy diary!

BIZZY: When she was on the toilet.

To BIZZY.

JAKEY: Okay son. Shut the fuck up now.

LEO: I need some water. I gotta get some water.

He opens the door and almost walks headlong into MICHAEL who has tea.

LEO: Oh Michael. Hello. That for us. Lovely. Nice cup of tea. Could do with that.

MICHAEL stares, his face grave. And then, as KATHERINE before…

MICHAEL: Moo.

Everything goes still for a few seconds. The men are quite stunned by this, and LEO feels like he's entered a new stage of his nightmare.

Moo.

Silence. But then MICHAEL's face creases with laughter. LEO stares.

MICHAEL: Sorry. My little joke. She told me all about it. Moo. Ha ha ha.
(*Silence.*) Come on boys. I was kidding around. Actually you're lucky. I meant to come in here and give you hell but things have been going rather well today.
The market.
Do my trading anywhere these days. Tent in the highlands; yacht in the Caribbean. Makes no difference. That's how I cut loose from the office today. Gave it to Katherine. She needed to get out. We swapped. She went to my office, I'm working next door.
So now you're dealing with a man.

JAKEY and LEO look at each other.

MICHAEL: (*To LEO.*) Sorry about before. Currency's doing cartwheels. I'm betting on the pound caving. Rollercoaster this morning, but I'm ahead. I'm well ahead. (*He checks his watch.*) Eight a.m. Twenty up. Good going eh?

Beat.

LEO: Oh yes. Absolutely.

JAKEY: What is it you do?

MICHAEL: Me? This and that. Background's banks. Banks, money – that's what I know. What do I do? Who can say. How deep do you want to go? Anyhow, everything's linked so what's it matter.

LEO: I see.

MICHAEL: Just a man. A working man. A man who works.

LEO: Right.

JAKEY: Twenty up eh?

MICHAEL: Twenty up.

JAKEY: Twenty. Phoo. Twenty…?

MICHAEL: Just for pressing buttons.
(*Laughs.*) Yep. It's gonna be a busy day. (*Beat.*)
Speaking of which… (*Claps hands together.*)
Let's talk about this thing shall we. Let's talk about the job in hand…the work…

LEO looks thoroughly miserable.

Who wants to get the ball rolling?

Beat.

Okay. Awkward silence. I was warned about that.

JAKEY: Look, mate…

MICHAEL: Yes?

LEO has to stop JAKEY.

LEO: I'm so sorry.

MICHAEL: Okay. Sorry. Yes.

JAKEY: No, we done nothing.

MICHAEL: Okay, yes, she said you'd done nothing.

JAKEY: No…I mean…

LEO: In all fairness…

JAKEY: …in all fairness, we done plenty. Take a look around. That look like nothing?

MICHAEL: Well, we'll come to that…

JAKEY: I mean, I know we're a few weeks over and that…

MICHAEL: Yes…

JAKEY: But at the same time, last few days we been going double-quick…

MICHAEL: Really? Double-quick?

JAKEY: Double-quick, absolutely. That's why her…her…

MICHAEL helping to midwife this sentence with his arms.

…flare-up…it threw us.

MICHAEL: Her flare-up, by which you mean…

JAKEY: …her outburst. Her…

MICHAEL: Her flare-up.

JAKEY: Her flare-up.

MICHAEL: So what exactly…prompted her…flare-up. Yesterday? From your point of view?

JAKEY: She…she…

LEO: I'm so terribly sorry.

JAKEY: Who can say? P'rhaps she's got things on her mind.

MICHAEL: Things on her mind. What sort of things?

JAKEY: Well, I mean…

MICHAEL: Three builders, no work sort of things?

He looks at BIZZY and goes into action.

JAKEY: Or maybe she's thinking of more important things, I don't know…

LEO shoves JAKEY away.

LEO: (*Hastily intervening.*) Really, I can't say enough how sorry I am.
Things have been on the slide for a while. These last few weeks, we've barely exchanged words. I don't know why. The conversation dried up. It wasn't like that at the start. At the start…

MICHAEL: Excuse me just one second…

MICHAEL dashes out the room. The builders are left alone. JAKEY and LEO stare at each other. JAKEY shakes his head. LEO appears to be seeking God somewhere in the ceiling. MICHAEL returns.

MICHAEL: Unbelievable. The market right now…thirty up…go on…'at the start…?'

Beat.

LEO: …oh when we first started coming here…

MICHAEL: Back at the dawn of time…(*He grins.*)…I'm
sorry.

LEO: …a while ago, yes…she was…she was cheerful and
lively in the mornings…(*Beat.*) You must understand,
We've not known a situation like this before.

MICHAEL: What, beautiful girl…work…

LEO: Well yes, she's very attractive but…

MICHAEL: I'm glad you think so.

LEO tries to assure MICHAEL of the purity of his intention.

LEO: Oh no what I mean is…

MICHAEL: Yes, what *do* you mean?

JAKEY butts in.

JAKEY: Yesterday was sort of the climax.
She came in here…and…well…I don't exaggerate, she
went on for ten minutes without coming up for air…just,
you know, throwing insults around and
everything…abusing us…

LEO: In fairness Jakey…

JAKEY: No, in fairness Leo…

MICHAEL: Perhaps she had good reason? Perhaps she felt
you were stretching out the work?

JAKEY: But that's just not the case…

MICHAEL: Because we were both wondering…

LEO: There *have* been these genuine hold-ups…

JAKEY: …authentic delays…

MICHAEL: ..building work sometimes seems to become…

JAKEY: Job's a job. You get it done. We wouldn't…

MICHAEL: …infinitely elastic…

JAKEY: It's not that. It's not elastic.

MICHAEL: Builders sometimes…

JAKEY: I refute that.

MICHAEL: …perhaps this whole project is a sort of literal…

JAKEY: …see, I don't think so…

MICHAEL: …a sort of literal representation of Xeno's paradox…

JAKEY: Nothing of the sort.

MICHAEL: (*Grandly.*) …the finish line you never reach.

JAKEY: Look! Michael. Look around you! Gawd. Some people. Look out your window. Turn on the telly. What do you see? Buildings. Who builds that stuff? Builders. We're a respectable trade. I don't see why we should all be treated like…

MICHAEL: But I'm not talking about builders *in general…*

Again, LEO sees the need to take over.

LEO: See…if we could somehow make amends…

MICHAEL: Ah…amends…yes…

LEO: Since she feels aggrieved.

MICHAEL: Feels? Yes. Katherine…As you know, she's wanted this…Quiet Space for some time. This…Sanctum Sanctorum.
And what Katherine wants.
I want.

Beat.

LEO: I understand.

JAKEY: Yeah, we've run over.

MICHAEL: By some margin.

JAKEY: Sometimes you run over. It happens.

MICHAEL: I understand. You run over, but now, see, now…

JAKEY: Nearly there you see Michael.

MICHAEL: …now, see, it's all about *completion*. Completion is very important to Katherine now. To both of us actually.

LEO: (*From within a nightmare.*) One big push. All that's needed. If we get some steam up.

MICHAEL: Some steam. Yes.

JAKEY: Course.

MICHAEL: So you're nearly done then?

JAKEY: We're nearly there.

MICHAEL: That's the main thing.

JAKEY: That's what I'm saying.

LEO: Get some steam up.

JAKEY: Just leave us to get on with it. Be lovely.

MICHAEL: Yes, but…when?

JAKEY: When?

MICHAEL: When.

JAKEY: Well look, I mean…

MICHAEL: *What* do you mean?

JAKEY: At this stage…

MICHAEL: Late stage…

JAKEY: At this late stage…

MICHAEL raises a hand.

MICHAEL: When?

JAKEY: See what you don't understand…

MICHAEL: Is there something I don't understand?

JAKEY: This sort of a job…

MICHAEL: Da da da da da.

Pause.

JAKEY: When you…

MICHAEL: Da da da da da.

Pause.

JAKEY: If…

MICHAEL: Da da da da…

Silence. JAKEY shrugs.

When?

JAKEY makes a few half hearted attempts to bullshit something.

JAKEY: That's the thing. You find out *when* by doing it.

Pause. Then slowly…anger flickering to the surface now and then.

MICHAEL: See…I'm not getting on too well with her. Just at the moment. And I think that's because of the work going on here. I think if the work were finished, we'd get on better. And the thing that makes it worse for me is that while we're not getting on…you're here…with her. With my Katherine. Every day. While I'm at my office. Or alone in my apartment. And I think, had we

79

been getting on better, she may have listened to me and fired you weeks ago. But Katherine…Katherine, she's very forgiving. You see.

Beat – JAKEY and BIZZY look at each other.

JAKEY: Mate…

MICHAEL: Mate?

JAKEY frowns, LEO steps in.

LEO: I swear to God Michael. This thing will be completed before the weekend. I swear to God it will..

MICHAEL: Ah. Clarity. Good. I like that. Very good. 'Before the weekend.'

JAKEY looks askance.

MICHAEL: Good. Let's have it in writing shall we?

LEO and JAKEY stare. MICHAEL walks across the room.

MICHAEL: Better in writing. Nothing personal. Helps focus the mind. If it's all right with you.

LEO: Of course.

MICHAEL: Lovely. Back in a tick.

He leaves the room.

JAKEY: Tosser. (*He paces.*) Little tosspot! What does he know? He knows nothing. *Nothing!*

LEO: Jakey…

JAKEY: Comes in. Made thirty in a morning. Thirty what? Groats?

LEO: For my sake…

JAKEY: No wonder she's not sure. No wonder she don't want to marry him.

LEO: Oh no. Jakey. Please.

JAKEY: No wonder she got herself out of that one. Married to this little git? I don't think so.

LEO: Jakey, inadmissible. Inadmissible. Illegally obtained.

JAKEY: Wake up morning after morning with that prat? No wonder she changed her mind. No wonder she lost her appetite.

LEO: For me Jakey. For me!

Enter MICHAEL, bearing a document.

MICHAEL: Here you are. If you just want to have a look at that and sign it. It's very straightforward.

Beat – JAKEY says nothing 'for Leo'.

Really, it's not a big deal. Just a pledge. To say if you're not done by the weekend, then…

JAKEY: Then what?

Beat.

MICHAEL: Then you forfeit your fee.

JAKEY: Christ Almighty.

MICHAEL: Fair?

JAKEY: Fair? What is this? Roots?

LEO stares at JAKEY.

LEO: Fit and fair Michael. Fit and fair.

JAKEY: What am I, picking cotton on his master's bleedin' plantation?

LEO: That's all right Jakey. We'll be all right. We'll get it done.

MICHAEL: All right?

LEO: Absolutely. It's just what we need round here. Some order.

MICHAEL: (*To JAKEY.*) Listen to the boss.

LEO: It's gone far enough.

LEO signs the document. JAKEY watches.

JAKEY: Order?
Here. I'll show you order.

He half guides, half pushes MICHAEL towards the wire.

Take a look at that. Go on. Get closer.

MICHAEL: What is it? Careful!

JAKEY: Have a smell. Go on. Smell it.

LEO: Jakey!

He releases MICHAEL.

MICHAEL: What is that thing?

JAKEY: Oh, nothing. Nothing. Just an instrument of torture in the corner waiting to kill us. But never mind about that.

MICHAEL: And why's it there? Why haven't you fixed it?

JAKEY: Why? Oh yes, why? Because we've not been allowed to. That's why! Because we can't switch off the electricity for half an hour.

MICHAEL: Oh come on…

JAKEY: Am I lying Leo?

MICHAEL: For half an hour? You expect me to believe that?

LEO: In our defence Michael, that's absolutely right. She's not let us disconnect the power.

JAKEY: Hunched up in there she's been. Day in, day out.

MICHAEL: Every day?

JAKEY: Every minute of every day.

MICHAEL stares at LEO.

LEO: All true. All true.

He puts his hand to his head.

MICHAEL: Oh God.
Then she's the same.
She really is the same.

Pause. JAKEY and LEO exchange looks. MICHAEL's head in his hands.

MICHAEL: (*From a depth of sadness.*) Oh God!

Beat.

LEO: It's from where we stripped the lights see.

MICHAEL silent. LEO and JAKEY look at each other again.

LEO: The inset wall lights.

MICHAEL: That girl.
That rare and difficult girl.

MICHAEL completely recovers.

Not once? She's not been out once?

LEO: Not while we've been here.

MICHAEL: Oh God.

LEO: Any chance us doing it now? Get some steam up.

Beat.

LEO: …while she's not here, could we…

MICHAEL: (*Impatient.*) Didn't you hear me. I can't have the power off..the market's going through the roof…I can't turn the power off now.

LEO: Fair enough.
(*Beat.*) See, in our defence…

JAKEY: You try working under these conditions. Threat of extinction hanging over you. Doesn't help the atmosphere. What about my kid? You thought about that have you?

MICHAEL: Your kid?

JAKEY: That's my bloody kid there! Oh I know what you think. Come in and sort out the clowns for your missis. That's not how it is chum.

MICHAEL: Hang on…

JAKEY: We haven't been able to get the paint on properly because of the subsidence.
(*He enthusiastically points out fresh cracks in the walls.*)
Look. Look. That went on yesterday. Already cracked. That's subsidence!
We warned her weeks ago but she said she'd had it sorted. Course, she had that other lot of monkeys in before. Pony they are. They're all wotsit's men. What's his name. The surveyor. (*Clicking fingers.*) Leo?

LEO: Fenwick.

JAKEY: Fenwick. He gets his own mugs in. They're notorious. They bungle everything.

MICHAEL examines the wall.

See it's all right her having a go at us, but we were told this was painting and decorating, not structural.

LEO: We've done a fair bit of structural…(work actually.)

JAKEY: Not that we can't do structural but we have to know…(what it is she wants.)

LEO: The fountains…

JAKEY: We got a death trap in the corner we can't fix. As for the paint issue…

LEO: In fairness, we had the whole room done emerald green after two weeks, then she changed her mind and opted for the yellow…

JAKEY: Then she changed her mind back, and then changed it again. I mean, course, we try an' be flexible…

MICHAEL: (*Inward.*) And then she changed her mind…yes…

Beat. JAKEY and BIZZY exchange looks.

JAKEY: She does seem very…*indecisive…*

Beat. JAKEY and LEO exchange looks.

MICHAEL: (*Inward.*) Indecisive. Yes. Yes.

JAKEY: She wants to do things herself, fine, but you gotta know the basics. She stopped us smoking right. She stopped us listening to the radio right. It's been like the bleedin' Taliban. I'm not complaining, but now…in flies America. We get another pasting from you.
We're just ordinary working men. You understand? We never had this problem before.

MICHAEL: No. No. Fair point. Fair point.

JAKEY senses the moment is right.

JAKEY: And you've obviously…*both* got things on your mind. Personal stuff. About love. (*MICHAEL looks up.*) It's all right. I can see. I can see it all.

LEO: (*Weakly.*) Anyway…

MICHAEL: What can you see? What do you mean *personal stuff?*

Beat.

JAKEY: I can just…see. I see it all. The whole situation. *Personal* stuff.

LEO: So what we need to do…

MICHAEL: What personal stuff? What are you talking about?

JAKEY: Oh, I mean…you can just see…

MICHAEL: See what?

JAKEY: What you're going through.

MICHAEL stares.

MICHAEL: And what exactly am I going through?

JAKEY: Eight, three, one.

Beat.

MICHAEL: Eight, three, one.

JAKEY: Eight letters. Three words. One meaning.

MICHAEL stares blankly.

I. Love. You.

Beat.

Caw, dear oh dear. Catch up.
Love.

MICHAEL: What about it?

JAKEY: I can see it's not right. You and her. She's…she's weighing things up…some decision.

MICHAEL: What decision?

JAKEY: Oh, a decision about a choice…

MICHAEL: A decision about a choice.

JAKEY: About you. Huge things. I can see it all. My mother was a gypsy. She loves you…not my mother. She's dead. Katherine. She loves you. I can see it..

MICHAEL stares.

LEO: Em…

MICHAEL: (*Wheeling round at LEO.*) Will you please belt up!

LEO: So sorry.

MICHAEL: How do you know she loves me?

JAKEY: See the way you know the market…

MICHAEL leans so far forward, it's like he'll topple over.

…I know the human heart.

MICHAEL: Is that so?

JAKEY: Oh yeah.

MICHAEL: So she loves me does she?

JAKEY: Oh yes.

MICHAEL: Really.

JAKEY: Very much.

MICHAEL: Well in that case, perhaps you'd like to explain why…(she changed her mind…etc.)

JAKEY: See you probably want to know why she turned down your proposal of marriage.

MICHAEL is rocked by this. LEO, unseen to MICHAEL, sits down in despair.

MICHAEL: How d'you know that? Did she tell you?

JAKEY: Not at all.

MICHAEL: (*Inward.*) She would never. How do you know?.

JAKEY: I see things very clearly.

MICHAEL: How do you know damn it !

JAKEY: Relax Michael. See…see…I'm looking at you. I'm looking at the room. The Quiet Space. I'm thinking… something sad. Something sad. I'm thinking…someone died…yes…someone…very close to Katherine…it's Katherine's thing…the room…the feeling…the feeling… feminine…feminine…her Mother…yes her mother died…and the room…the room…that's where she wants to come and…dwell…but…where does that leave you… and I'm thinking…you were…are…were/are…in love… it was going well…it was passionate, exciting…you asked her to marry you…she accepted…and then her mum died…and Katherine…she was…affected…she clammed up, changed…her feelings changed…she didn't know herself…didn't know her own body…she panicked…she backed off…off…she changed her mind! Indecision. Indecision. (*Triumphantly.*) She changed her mind and turned you down and you still don't know why!

MICHAEL: (*Suddenly standing.*) Stop it!

He walks over to the window.

How did you know that? (*Pause.*) I've been in misery. One minute she's marrying me, the next she won't see me. Three months! Three months it's been since I was here. (*He points next door.*) That bed. The smell of it. The smell of her. That's the closest I've come to my former wife-to-be.

He catches himself.

How did you know?

JAKEY: It's just in the air.

JAKEY and MICHAEL stare. MICHAEL accepts the bait.

MICHAEL: See, my line of work...we're remote...we're cut off...banking.
I don't work with my hands – like you. I work with my head. I think things through.
(*Beat.*) Katherine. (*Beat.*) I don't know if my Katherine will ever come back.

JAKEY: Come back? How d'you mean?

MICHAEL: I've been making good money for a decade.
Keeping ahead of the pack.
Work's been the priority.
I thought if, by some miracle, I could fit love in as well, so much the better, but I wouldn't let it take over my time: I've seen other people do that, and lose ground because of it.
And then Katherine came along.
She opened my eyes to everything. (*Beat.*) I'd always taken life for granted.
She made me see it was a gift.
She made life worth living.
(*Beat.*) Course I had to win her first. Against tough competition. (*Beat.*) But I enjoyed that.
The battle just made her more desirable.
(*Beat.*) You know how I won her?

Beat.

Nothing complicated.
So simple.
So natural.
Love. It ran through me like a train. Direct. Intercity. No stops. Took me straight to her. I didn't want to be

anywhere else. With other girls, an evening in's worse than death, but with Katherine, I actually looked forward to it.

(*Beat.*) Oh Katherine.

He looks up at JAKEY.

Sounds like a children's story doesn't it. [(*Beat.*) Well there was a grown-up side to it too.

JAKEY grins.

I'd heard these things about Katherine which sort of gave her a mystique if you like. She had a bit of a reputation at work. But till I actually got her home, I had no idea what a package she was.

We'd been to see *A Streetcar Named Desire.*

It's a play.

I wanted her to think I had interests outside work. She loved that character. Stanley Kowalski. I thought he was an idiot, but for some reason, he appealed to her.

We sat and talked and then went back to my apartment.

We hadn't even touched hands but she seemed strangely overheated. She was wearing a leather skirt and her top was done up just a bit too tight.

In the kitchen, I had four bottles of Margaux.

In the living room, I have a fish tank where I keep my tropical fish.

We sat down. I didn't know what to expect. For some reason I was shaking. She opened her bag and took out what I took to be a make-up compact, but it wasn't...

MICHAEL smiling. JAKEY waiting. Pause. Almost a tableau.

LEO: That's it Bizzy. Up and down. Nice and smooth. Good lad.

LEO proceeds with his tasks.

MICHAEL: She came and sat beside me.

MICHAEL sits back and smiles then leans forward and whispers in JAKEY's ear.

JAKEY: Oh my God!

More whispering.

JAKEY: You're putting me on!

MICHAEL: I kid you not.

JAKEY: With the tropical fish!

LEO and BIZZY stop work and look up. LEO tries to steer BIZZY back.

LEO: Good grout this. Not my usual brand.

JAKEY: She never!

LEO: Takes nicely to the wall. Comes off clean.

MICHAEL: You see!

JAKEY: I do now.

LEO: Bizzy, your brush lad. It's dripping on the floor. That's it.

MICHAEL new energy.

MICHAEL: Before I'd met this girl, I'd allowed two hours a day in my schedule for love- you may laugh, (*No one does.*)...but two hours in my job, it's not a joke.
Two hours a day.
I thought it would be enough, but it wasn't even close.
No schedule could hold the force between us. She.
Katherine My mighty Katherine. Two hours weren't enough for Katherine. Four hours. Ten. Twenty.
Not all the hours of daylight nor all the hours of darkness were enough for Katherine.
I had to give myself to her. Do anything she said! The passion of this woman knew no bounds.

She wanted to escape her body; to be crushed; to snuff out that need inside. You couldn't touch her without feeling it; everything that was bottled up behind that too tightly fitting top...the tension, the anger, the fear – it all erupted when she let that voracious appetite loose.

After two months, I found myself asking her to marry me. It was the first thing I'd ever done without thinking. She accepted immediately. Of course she would. I craved every married minute with her. Hungered.

It was the happiest day of my life.

Beat.

Then it all went wrong.

(*Beat.*) Her mother. Wasn't her fault. Not at all. (*Beat.*) She died.

(*Beat.*) Long battle with Cancer.

Well, you can't factor *that* in can you.

(*Beat.*) I knew she and Katherine were close, but I...I didn't know it would affect her so badly.

I thought...I thought she'd be sad for a few days...a few weeks...and then...yunno...forget about it...get on with life.

If you'd told me that everything between us would crumble into dust, I'd've laughed in your face.

But that's exactly what happened.

New energy.

She decided she wanted to *live cleanly.*

The lights went out inside her and she became repulsed by everything *physical.*

This incredible *physical* woman was suddenly consumed by a gigantic and useless *spiritual* side.

People told me that sometimes when someone dies this happens. Especially with girls and mothers. They sort of get a bit wrapped up in it all.

I told myself it was a passing phase. Might last a week or two, but no more.

I've never been so wrong.

Every day, she was less in this world, and more in some other tuneless, dull one.

I said to myself 'she's grieving, she's grieving, that's what it is.' But to be honest, I was just repeating things I'd read in *Cosmopolitan* and the article never said how it ended.

Or when.

It just towed the usual line about patience and understanding But that wasn't how our relationship was.

Patience. Understanding.

Fuck all that, we had so much more!

Do you know what I mean?

JAKEY: I do Michael.

MICHAEL: But Katherine was getting worse.

She started to see mystery in everything. Signs. She started to make observations about the universe. About life and death and why things happen.

She'd pull out a crisp from a packet and claim it had the face of someone she knew. Then she'd spend the week trying to work out its meaning.

If a gust of wind got up while she was on the phone, it had special significance. If she mislaid a photo, it held a secret message.

She talks about... about fish having souls. Fish. And vegetables. And trees. Trees. And dust, and rain and wind...everything...everything in her damned tuneless universe has a soul except for me!

Oh no. Not me.

She told me she didn't want to marry me. She returned the ring I'd given her and asked me not to see her.

Asked me not to see her. That girl!

(*Beat.*) I thought I had her for keeps.

(*Beat.*) That gentle lovely pale English rose makes me feel so dark and earthy and alive.

Beat.

Every day, every damned day she's on about this Quiet Space and the damned builders and what they've done and what they haven't done. Oh yes. She'll phone me. I can't see her, but she'll phone all right. And I answer as patiently...as manfully...as cordially as I can.

Yesterday she threw up her hands in despair and called for me to come.

She needed me.

My passionate pale English rose...left a key for me under the mat.

So here I am.

MICHAEL looks up and recovers himself.

Well then, here I am.

He looks around trying to locate himself.

JAKEY: Here we are.

He looks at JAKEY and then at LEO and BIZZY working. He goes to the contract that LEO's signed.

MICHAEL: I'm holding you up.

JAKEY shrugs.

You have to work.

Beat.

What am I doing? (*Beat.*) See with Katherine...with Katherine...(*He taps his head.*) I lose my bearings. (*He shrugs.*) I love her. That's how it is. Love makes you crazy. Yes. (*Beat.*) Yes.

Beat – uncomfortable.

Well anyway...she'll...she'll be back later...
...to review the work. You'd better press on.

JAKEY: Okey doke.

MICHAEL: Great.

Beat.

JAKEY: Good to get that off your chest.

MICHAEL: Yes. (*Beat.*) Off my chest. Course. (*Beat.*) Right. I should let you…

He leaves and immediately re-enters.

Right.

MICHAEL nods, then leaves and returns.

You get it don't you.

JAKEY: Course.

MICHAEL: Good-oh.

Leaves and returns.

A man thing. You have to make your mind up. You can't just drift.

JAKEY: Absolutely.

MICHAEL: Absolutely.

Beat.

Or you're lost.

JAKEY: Absolutely.

MICHAEL: Good-oh.

Pause.

A love thing. That's the bottom line.

JAKEY: Course..

MICHAEL: Of course. (*Beat.*) Right then.

MICHAEL leaves. JAKEY stands idle while LEO works. JAKEY opens and shuts the door, checking where he's gone.

JAKEY: Not getting any. There y'are. Three words.

Thinks.

Getting none. Two words. (*Thinks.*) Prat. One word.

He shakes his head.

Some people.

Looks up.

Eh Leo.

LEO ignores him.

So there I am, staring into her Quiet Space, up comes her mate. I'm assuming nothing, lo and behold, off comes Mini number two, I'm thinking, aye aye, Three's Up Mother Brown.

LEO: (*Calm and without turning.*) We're going to finish this ruddy job and leave.
Bizzy. Just copy the patterns I'm making on the other wall.
Jakey, the beading already has an adhesive on the back. Position it round the indentations on the surface, and we'll go over it with a light coat of paint. Don't smudge the patterns. Let the paint go on sparingly. The pattern's quite delicate you see. It's a copy of a pattern from an Isalmic temple in Istanbul.

JAKEY: Anything you say Leo.

LEO: That's it Bizzy. Just like that. You've got it.
Don't rush, that's the main thing. They're lovely patterns these. I drove up to Reading for them especially.
Simple you see. Beautiful and simple. That's it Bizzy.

JAKEY looks over at BIZZY. The son has actually been making good progress. JAKEY smiles.

JAKEY: That's it Biz. Caw, you're good at that. Ain't chou.

Beat.

He likes the patterns. He's like one of those mongs off the telly. Ha ha. Aren't you Biz. Ha ha.

Beat.

Let's get out of here . Never mind tomorrow. We could do this in a day? Friday off. Long weekend. Toast in bed.

LEO no comment.

I mean it Leo, imagine that eh? Toast in bed.

LEO: Please Jakey. I beg of you, don't torment me. I have my limits.

JAKEY: I'm not. I mean it. Come on Leo. We could do this in a day. No problem.

LEO: (*Solemnly.*) Are you really serious?

JAKEY: One hundred per cent.

LEO: If we put our backs into it... then perhaps.

JAKEY: Then let's do that. Eh Biz?
Come on Leo. Long weekend. Lovely. I've had enough. I want to get out of here. House-a-bleedin bondage. Him 'n' her. Some people.

LEO: I'm ruddy angry with you Jakey.

JAKEY: Oh Leo. No! Don't be angry.

LEO: I'm ruddy angry.

JAKEY: Very ruddy, or just ruddy?

LEO: You take advantage.

JAKEY puts an arm round him.

JAKEY: Leo.

LEO just shakes his head. JAKEY laughs.
BIZZY drifts towards the wire.

JAKEY: I mean it. Let's motor. Really motor. Get out
tonight. Go home.

BIZZY: I know what he said in your ear.

JAKEY: Yeah, all right Biz. (*To LEO.*)
All that yellow. It's starting to smell funny.

LEO: You really mean it?

JAKEY: Really mean it Leo.

BIZZY: She understands everything.

LEO: We'll have to put our backs into it.

JAKEY: Good. Fine. Whatever. That's what I want. I'm in
the mood. I've got a passion for it. A hunger. What about
you Bizzy?

And BIZZY is staring at the wire thinking 'Shall I try it.'

Bizzy, you don't need to do the beading over there.

BIZZY: I couldn't have a girl like that.

LEO: Bizzy son. Come out the danger zone would you.

BIZZY lifts up his arm.

JAKEY: Bizzy, what you doing. Don't touch that!

LEO: Bizzy! What you doing?!!

JAKEY: Bizzy, no!

LEO: Bizzy!

*BIZZY reaches up to the live-wire and accordingly receives
an electric shock.*

Black.

Dramatic purposeful music.

Part III

Black.

Music clicks off with – spotlight on JAKEY.

Is it funereal or stagey – the atmosphere is uncertain at first. The rest of the stage as shadowy and indistinct as possible.

He begins slowly, in a sort of 'are-you-sitting-comfortably' sort of way.

JAKEY: I had a mate up in Whitechapel.
Plumber he was. Couldn't bring his wife to the boil. No matter what he did, it never happened in the cot. He bought books. Followed diagrams. I think he even took a course, but it was always the same. Push, prod, suck, bang. Goodnight. She was bored out her skin. And, being a woman, she eventually had to say something.

Tight spot to other side of the stage. LEO. Working. Laughing.

So my chap, Terry he was called, he feels rotten when she's told him.
He's half thought he didn't have the sparkle, but he's no idea he's that bad till she's said it to his face.
So when he's found out, he's reacted like any sensible man would in his predicament.
He's popped off down the pub for a drink.

LEO laughs.

So he drinks for an hour and a half, give or take, not long, but the time he's there, he's done sixteen pints of stout…
He's entered the premises at ten, he's left at eleven thirty…Leo, he's done two gallons in ninety minutes.

LEO laughs.

So he's gone down the underground catch a train home.
He's on the platform. Realises he's not had a slash.
Sixteen pints, hasn't had a slash right.
No sooner's he had the thought, he starts to feel the
weight of all that drink. He's stood there like a cow
waiting to be milked. I mean the man's *full to bursting*.
He has to piss or I don't know what.
So Terry's a bit drunk, but he's not lost his dignity – so
there's no way he's going in his kecks. And it's way too
far back up to the street. So instead, what he does, he
whips out his Vic and Bob and he starts to have a slash,
only, the platform's crowded with late night commuters.
But he don't care, he's letting it all out and there's anger
there. Real anger. He's pissing with a vengeance.
It's Niagara Falls on the Bakerloo.
Now Terry could put out forest fires with what's in him.
He could police a riot with what's coming out. And
suddenly, he starts enjoying himself. He starts whirling
around like a ballerina, making shapes in the air. Taking
aim. Picking out targets…button-holes, rings on fingers,
mobile phones, and he's giving himself points when he
hits. Round and round he's spinning, like a dervish, and
there's tourists, there's people coming back from the
theatre. Ravers. They're all caught in it. Round and
round. Gangs of kids. Rumanian beggars. It's chaos.
Everyone's running and ducking for cover. And Terry's
shouting; he's letting out his frustration…'this is for what
you did and this is for what you did' and talking crazy
talk blaming everyone for his unhappiness at home. Two
minutes go by, he's still going on; three minutes, no sign
of surrender.

LEO quietly crying with laughter.

Four minutes, I'm telling you Leo, four minutes.. but
now there's something else…

Hush.

He's stood on the edge of the platform and his stream of piss crosses the live track.

Pause.

Two and a half thousand volts of locomotive electricity pass instantly up Terry's little man.
Does it kill him? No.
Does he fall over? No.
Does he stop pissing?
Yes. He stops pissing.
A train arrives. No one bothers him. He gets on. He travels home like nothing's happened.
He's unaffected.
Two and a half thousand volts of electricity up his Sir Alex, and Terry's not affected.
Gets home. Let's himself in. Looks a state. Smells rotten. All's quiet. Goes upstairs to bed. Undresses. Has a scratch. Gets in the cot with his old dear. Falls asleep.

Hush.

Middle of the night, he wakes up.
He's had this unbelievable dream. He's got this power coming up through his loins. This urgent powerful force that he feels right down deep. And it's beautiful. He opens his eyes. His old dear's on top of him, and get this…she looks twenty years younger.
And she's in *ecstasy.* I mean she's going *stir friggin' crazy.* He thinks he's dreaming, but this is real. She's grinding up and down on him like a rodeo cowgirl. Pushing him into the cot. Shouting, screaming stuff out. She's foaming at the mouth. Her limbs are all over the place. He's thinking, 'what have I done.' But he's not in control of it. So he just starts to enjoy himself and pretty soon, he's feeling like he did on that underground platform, he's got that exact same feeling, and he's screaming the place down too.

After ninety minutes. Ninety minutes being eighty seven more minutes than the night of their honeymoon…she collapses like an old chimney. She looks up at him, just says 'thank-you.' And he says 'my pleasure' and tells her he loves her.

And that, Leo, Bizzy…that is why you don't see much of my mate Terry no more.

LEO: (*Finishing off.*) Marvellous. Marvellous. Eh Bizzy? You hear that eh?

Lights up. No sign of BIZZY…
And the room is transformed –
The sheets are off and what's there resembles a fabulous film set depicting the Garden of Eden – but not too camp – there is something indisputably tasteful and well-done about the thing. There should be some lovely ornate Alhambresque patterning to admire on one of the walls. This is a genuine achievement.
Only the wire still jars.

LEO: I think that's it.

LEO and JAKEY take it all in. There is wonder.

I do. I think that's it. Look at that. It's magnificent.

JAKEY: It's pretty good. It's pretty eff-ing good. Bizzy?

LEO: Bizzy!

JAKEY: Come on son. Have a look.

Silence.

Bizzy!

A voice from somewhere.

BIZZY: What?

JAKEY: Come out here. See what we've done. All of us together.

Silence.

JAKEY: Bizzy!

BIZZY: Will I be impotent?

JAKEY: Course you won't.

BIZZY: What if I am?

JAKEY: You won't be all right.

Beat.

BIZZY: How d'you know?

JAKEY: Well I don't. But let's not worry for now shall we?

Beat.

Come on Biz! Come and have a look!

BIZZY: My eyes hurt.

JAKEY and LEO exchange looks.

LEO: Shouldn't he see someone?

JAKEY: He's all right. He's fine. Here y'are Biz. Wear these. (*He takes a pair of shades from a back pocket and tosses them over to invisible BIZZY.*) It was just a little shock that's all. Won't do you no harm.

Silence.

BIZZY: Can we go home now?

JAKEY: In a minute son. Why don't you come out here and see what we've done eh?

BIZZY: My hair feels funny.

JAKEY: Yer hair is funny pube-head. Get out here. Come on!

Rustling…and BIZZY emerges, shades on, hair on end like in a cartoon. JAKEY and LEO stifle laughter.

JAKEY: (*Hammy.*) I throw the switch and give my creation life!

LEO laughs.

BIZZY: I'm not coming.

He goes back to his hide-out.

JAKEY: Oh don't be so sensitive.

LEO: Poor little lad! Come on Bizzy.

JAKEY: Come here.

LEO: Well done son. You did marvellous. (*BIZZY stays out.*) You did. Terrific job. You all right now? Feeling better?

JAKEY: He's all right. You're all right aren't you?

BIZZY: Yeah.

JAKEY laughs despite himself.

JAKEY: I'm sorry Biz.

He laughs some more.

You want my comb?

BIZZY: It won't stay down.

Putting his hand in his hair.

JAKEY: Never mind. It suits you.

BIZZY pulls a face. JAKEY pulls him towards him.

JAKEY: Come 'ere. Let's have a look at you.

Holding his chin and staring into his eyes.

Watch my hand.

Moves hand left to right checking eye movement.

JAKEY: Blind. Oh well.

BIZZY: Will I be impotent?

Beat.

JAKEY: Yes. You'll be impotent, which is a shame cause everyone's after your genes. Ha ha.

BIZZY: Will I?

JAKEY: No course you won't. That's why I told you 'bout my friend Terry.

BIZZY: Yeah but you made that up.

JAKEY: I never.

BIZZY: You did!

JAKEY: How can you say that!

BIZZY: Cause you did!

JAKEY: All true. Every word.

BIZZY: (*Laughing.*) He weren't pishing on the underground and 'at.

JAKEY: You calling me a liar?

BIZZY: Yes.

JAKEY: All true. Every word of it.

BIZZY: Weren't.

JAKEY: Bizzy!

BIZZY: Like you said mum was staying. That weren't true neither.

JAKEY: Hang on. I thought it was when I said it.

BIZZY: Yeah but it wasn't was it.

JAKEY: Bizzy! (*Beat.*) I got that wrong. I made a mistake. (*Beat.*) People are funny.

BIZZY: You said she weren't going nowhere. You promised.

JAKEY: I didn't know she was did I.

BIZZY: But you promised.

JAKEY: (*Laughing.*) What happened? You always thought I was the greatest.

BIZZY: No I didn't.

JAKEY: I remember you did. What happened?

BIZZY: I thought you was a lying bullshitting bastard.

LEO: (*Disappointment.*) Oh no now Bizzy.

JAKEY: (*Hurt.*) Right, well thanks Biz.

LEO: He didn't mean it.

BIZZY laughs heartily.

BIZZY: I did.

JAKEY: No, that's not funny. That's not nice. (*BIZZY laughs.*) No, that's not a joke. That hurts, right. That hurts me.

BIZZY's face falls when he realises JAKEY isn't laughing.

BIZZY: Sorry.

JAKEY: You see.

BIZZY: Sorry.

JAKEY: Makes me feel sick what you said there. (*Beat.*) Thinking that's what you thought all that time.

(*BIZZY just shuffles about. Silence.*) Really makes me feel sick. (*Beat.*)

BIZZY: Be good if I'm impotent won't it.

JAKEY looks hard at BIZZY.

JAKEY: Oy!

BIZZY: What?

JAKEY: Don't do that.

BIZZY: What?

JAKEY: Don't go from all high-spirits-n-laughy to all down-in-the dumps right.

BIZZY doesn't know what to do.

JAKEY: Come here. You're all right. You're a good kid. (*BIZZY stares. JAKEY rubs his hair.*) You're all right Biz. (*Indicating the room.*) Look what we done eh? Whatddya think?

BIZZY: Yeah.

JAKEY: (*Nodding.*) Yeah.
What we can do in a day! Think about that eh? You do that in a day, what you gonna do your whole life eh Biz?

BIZZY: Loads of it.

JAKEY: Fuckin' loads of it!

They laugh.

LEO: My God. I'm all in.

JAKEY: Look at it though.
Will you look. At. This. Nonsense.

Shakes his head.

LEO: Her Quiet Space.

JAKEY: Her Quiet Space. (*Shakes head.*) Some people.
(*Beat.*) Just the wire to go.

LEO: Our old friend.

JAKEY: Then…

LEO: Get down The Plough. Jerry's opening late.

JAKEY: Oh those three words.
'Jerry's opening late.'

LEO: Wait for Michael. (*He checks his watch.*) Five minutes
he said. Get the power off. Tuck it in. Smooth it off. You
wanna go on? I don't mind. I'll do it myself.

JAKEY: Don't be daft Leo. We'll all chip in.

BIZZY: We can all help out.

LEO: All right. Okay.

JAKEY: Can't wait to see her face.

LEO: Oh yeah. That'll be nice.

JAKEY: Listen to him take all the credit. (*Beat.*) That's what
smarts. She'll think it was down to him.

LEO: Well to some extent I suppose it was.

JAKEY: Bollocks. All he did was moan on about her. (*Beat.*)
Katherine. Bit of a girl our Katherine. Funny.

BIZZY: I want a girl like her.

JAKEY stares.

JAKEY: Oh no you don't Biz.

BIZZY: I do.

JAKEY: You want someone nice and easy with a big bright
smile.

BIZZY: I want Katherine.

JAKEY looks at LEO.

JAKEY: See Biz, what I think is, you like her cause you read her diary so you feel like you know her.

BIZZY: I do know her.

JAKEY: Fair enough, but that's cheating, see. You have to get girls to tell you what they're thinking *without* cheating.

BIZZY: How'd you do that?

JAKEY: Oh Biz...*that's* the question. That's the big big question. How d'you get those lovely lovely girls to want you and adore you and go wild about you.

BIZZY: How?

JAKEY: Well first off, you don't carry on like a freak. You act normal right Biz. You say nice things. Nice things or funny things doesn't matter. Funny things is better, then when they're laughing you say nice things all right.

BIZZY: Yeah.

BIZZY stares. JAKEY rubs his hair again.

JAKEY: Coming down the Plough with us? Have a bev?

BIZZY: All right.

JAKEY: All right.

Beat.

JAKEY: See. You can be normal can't you eh?

BIZZY: (*Beaming.*) Yeah.

JAKEY: Yeah.

Indicating next door.

LEO: Should I just…check…

JAKEY: Better not.

LEO: Better leave him.

JAKEY: Better had.

LEO starts to laugh, shaking his head.

JAKEY: What?

LEO just can't describe it.

LEO: The last couple of days. Just thinking. Ha ha ha.

JAKEY: Ha ha ha ha.

LEO: Ha ha ha ha.

JAKEY: Ha ha ha ha.

BIZZY: Ha ha ha.

JAKEY: Moo.

Laughter all round.

LEO: (*Fighting back tears.*) Moo.

More laughter.

Look though. Seriously, boys…I…I know we had our ups and downs…

JAKEY: Here we go.

LEO: Seriously Jakey…and there've been times when I…when I wondered if I wasn't with the two…

JAKEY: Steady…

LEO: …most abysmal delinquents on the planet…(*Laughter.*)

JAKEY: Leo!

LEO: …or if I wasn't trapped in some diabolical endless nightmare…

JAKEY: Heh!

LEO: …but…hear me out…I'm really so proud of you. I am. When the crunch came, you pulled out the stops. That's good enough for me.

JAKEY: Got some steam up.

LEO: Got some…(*He laughs.*) You little piss-taker.

JAKEY: What?

LEO: You know what! You little…(*He shakes his head.*)

JAKEY: Some people.

LEO: Some people.

JAKEY laughs.

JAKEY: You wanna fag.

LEO looks concerned.

Stop worrying all the time.

LEO: Go on then.

LEO takes one.

JAKEY: Fag Biz?

With BIZZY'S finger on the filter.

Wait…

BIZZY: What?

JAKEY: Bless the room bless the room.

LEO laughs.

Come on. Hands together.

JAKEY brings their hands together.

Right. Ready?

He looks up.

Old Lady in the tree…may this room…

LEO: …not collapse in the next half hour.

Laughter.

JAKEY: Show him the fountains Leo. You wanna see the fountains Biz?

BIZZY: Yeah.

JAKEY: Go on. Get 'em on.

LEO: All right. All right. Here we go.

JAKEY: Here we go. Watch this Biz.

LEO cautiously approaches a power switch front left and flicks it. Water bubbles through the pipes and up through the fountains.

LEO and JAKEY: Wahayyy.

JAKEY: Eh Biz?

BIZZY smiles.

BIZZY: Wahaaaaay!

JAKEY: Isn't it!

LEO: What about that then.

JAKEY: (*Laughing.*) Terrible.

LEO: It works.

JAKEY: How shit are we and it works. Ha ha ha.

LEO: You said to me, 'what did she ask for?' This is it.

(*Beat.*) Muslim wall-work. Ornamental fountains.
Statuesque representations of the elephant god Ganesh-a.

JAKEY: It's not just new lino is it Leo.

*LEO is making himself comfortable on the floor with a bag
under his head.*

LEO: It's more than new lino Jakey.

JAKEY: Award winningly shite.

LEO laughs and settles himself down.

LEO: Oy. Steady.

JAKEY: What you doing ?

LEO: I gotta lie down. I'm done in Jakey.

JAKEY: That's all right. You have a lie down. You deserve
it.

LEO: Can't keep my eyes open.

JAKEY: I mean, if you want, we'll wait, you go off…

LEO: No no. It's fine.

Beat.

JAKEY: You been working like a dog haven't you.

LEO: It's been a busy year.

Pause.

JAKEY: When was your last day off eh?

LEO: (*Laughing.*) Oh, a long while ago.

JAKEY: The Tropics. You gotta get to the Tropics. Do you
good. Sun. Hot sand. (*Beat.*) Different way of doing
things. Slow. We got a lot to learn from the Tropics.

LEO: Too old to change my ways now.

JAKEY: Bloody hell Leo, I'm only talking 'bout an holiday.

LEO smiles and shakes his head.

LEO: There's the expense…

JAKEY: You pay for it. *Afford* it later.

LEO: I like to keep within my means see.

JAKEY: Course you do. Course you do.

LEO: Can't help it.

JAKEY: Course you can't.

LEO: Just the way I am.
Here lies Leo. Always too old to change his ways.
Never quite got enough steam up.
(*Beat.*) Never quite the man he hoped he'd be.

Pause.

JAKEY: Yeah well…
(*Beat.*) You only need to buy a ticket.

LEO: Oh yes.

Beat.

JAKEY: Remember when I had the business. Had money then. Rolling in it.

LEO: Another little dip in the petty cash.

JAKEY laughs.

JAKEY: Mine to take it was!

Beat.

That was a giggle weren't it. The selling. Shop floor. Customers. I liked it. Makin' 'em laugh. All them gimmicks at Christmas.

LEO: Gimmicks all year.

JAKEY: Every month. That's right.

Allbright's Massive February Sale. This time we're really really closing down. Ha ha ha.

Beat.

Allbright's Massive March Sale – we're fucking off for good. (*Beat.*) That jumped-up prat in the bank! Remember him? Clueless!
Bloody country, locking someone up for selling a bed? People don't believe me when I tell 'em. What's that all about? Damn bloody country. (*Beat.*) I didn't know. Did I know you couldn't trade.(*Beat.*) I didn't know. What is *insolvent?* We had customers. I sold a bloody bed. Making a living I was. Not cheating no one.

BIZZY: What is 'insolvent?'

JAKEY: Insolvent. It's nothing.

Pause.

Christ.

BIZZY: You always say about the shop.

Pause.

JAKEY: Weeeell. (*Beat.*) Was a good shop.

BIZZY: Yeah but you always say about it.

JAKEY: Rabbiting on.
(*Beat.*) Yeah. (*Beat.*)
You done well kid. I'm proud of you.

BIZZY: Thanks.

Beat.

JAKEY: We'll get you onto mosaics next. You'll be good at that.

Pause.

BIZZY: Will mum see it?

JAKEY: What this…?

BIZZY: My work?

JAKEY: (*Beat: laughing.*)
No. No she won't.

BIZZY: Can't I show her?

JAKEY: No. You can't.

BIZZY: Why not?

JAKEY: Cause it's here and your mum don't know these people.

BIZZY: I'd like to show her.

JAKEY: Well, sometimes you can't have what you want Biz.

Pause.

BIZZY: Why can't I see mum?

JAKEY: (*Sleepily.*) Ohhh…coz she's busy.

Pause.

BIZZY: No *I'm* Bizzy.

Pause.

JAKEY: Yeah.
(*Beat.*) Nice one kid.

Beat.

BIZZY: She thinks I'm useless dun't she.

Beat.

JAKEY: Yeah. I think she must. Coz that's how she treats you. But I'm sure if she'd seen what you done 'ere, she'd change her mind.

Beat.

BIZZY: Why's she think I'm useless?

JAKEY: I doesn't matter what anyone thinks. It just
matters what you think. And you know you ain't useless
don't you.
(*Beat.*) Don't you.

BIZZY: Yeah.

Beat.

JAKEY: (*Sotto.*) Saw her down the Brick the other day doin'
all sorts Leo.

No response. He has a look but LEO's fallen asleep.

Leo's gone to sleep Bizzy.

He stares out the window.

BIZZY: Dad.

JAKEY: Yeah?

BIZZY: You know them two black girls you 'ad.

JAKEY: Oh yeah.

BIZZY: Was one of them mum?

Pause. JAKEY stares at BIZZY.

JAKEY: No Bizzy.

Beat.

BIZZY: That's good.

JAKEY: Your mum was my special girl.
(*Beat.*) My special girl she was.
(*Beat.*) Look at that. Big red sunset. Look how red it is.

*And indeed a deep dark red is pouring in through the
windows.*

Trouble with this country. Sun comes out when it's setting.

BIZZY and JAKEY stare at the sun each with their thoughts, then MICHAEL pokes his head round the door.

MICHAEL: Hi. Hi. (*He enters.*) Wow. Fabulous. Fabulous.

JAKEY: All right.

MICHAEL: Fabulous. Fabulous.

JAKEY: Whaddya think?

MICHAEL takes a look around.

MICHAEL: Amazing. I think she'll like it. She'll be back soon.

JAKEY nods.

JAKEY: Oh good. ·

MICHAEL: Oh good. Yeah. (*Beat.*) It's been a long time. For me.

JAKEY: Oh yeah. It has hasn't it.

MICHAEL stares.

JAKEY: Good day at the races?

MICHAEL: Races? Right. Yeah. The market. Actually, yes it was. Levelled out about tea-time. Finished the day fifty up.

JAKEY: Fifty eh.

MICHAEL: It doesn't all go to me. The Consultancy takes a share. A chunk. A big chunk.

JAKEY: But still. (*Beat.*) Fifty.

MICHAEL: Yeah. It's been a pretty good day.

JAKEY: Good.

MICHAEL takes a look round.

MICHAEL: Yes.
(*Beat.*) See I knew, if I you signed something, you'd get it done.

JAKEY: Oh yeah.

Beat.

Shame she never signed anything eh?

MICHAEL uncomfortable laugh.

Like the registry.

MICHAEL: Yes yes. I got it.

JAKEY: Nail her down. Book a band.

MICHAEL: So anyway…I'm done now. You can turn off the electricity.

JAKEY: Oh. Great.

Pause.

MICHAEL: Yeah, so if you want to do that …

JAKEY: Right away Michael. (*No movement.*)

Beat.

MICHAEL: See, when Katherine gets home…(*Beat.*) I want it to be, you know, just the two of us.

JAKEY: You and me?

MICHAEL: (*Politely indulgent.*) Me and Katherine.

JAKEY: Oh right.

MICHAEL: Yep.

JAKEY: That's a pity.

MICHAEL: Why's that then?

JAKEY: Be nice to see her reaction. After all this time.

MICHAEL: Haven't you had enough of her reactions.

JAKEY: Yeah but…you know what I mean. See how she reacts now.

MICHAEL: I'm sorry. It's best it's just the two of us.

JAKEY: You and her.

MICHAEL: Okay?

JAKEY with his thoughts.

JAKEY: Yeah course.

No movement.

MICHAEL: Great. So if you just want to …

JAKEY: Move along…

MICHAEL: Get on with the wire…

JAKEY: Better have it in writing.

Beat – again, polite acknowledgment of the joke.

MICHAEL: Will you start making preparations then?

JAKEY: No problem at all Michael.

MICHAEL: Great.

MICHAEL stares.

MICHAEL: I don't know how you got me talking earlier. I'm so sorry.

JAKEY: You must've wanted to.

MICHAEL: No. See, no. I didn't. (*Beat.*) It was private.

JAKEY: Very.

MICHAEL: Yes.

JAKEY: The tropical fish.

MICHAEL checks his watch.

MICHAEL: Right then. Get the big lad on his feet shall we?

He goes to rouse LEO, stands over him.

Come on soldier. Time to go home.

LEO doesn't stir.

Come on. You gotta do the electric wire.

Stands over.

Come on.

Then crouches.

Come on mate.

He rolls LEO around a bit. Sense of panic.

All right. Come on. What's the matter with him?

JAKEY: You don't have to prod him.

MICHAEL: He's not moving.

JAKEY: He's not cattle either.

MICHAEL: You do it then.

Pause.

JAKEY: Leo?

MICHAEL: Why isn't he moving?

JAKEY: Leo?

MICHAEL: Come on Leo. Time to go!

JAKEY: Heh, Leo.

MICHAEL: Wake up. Wake up. Come on. What's the matter!

JAKEY: Leo? (*JAKEY gets a panic.*) Leo?

MICHAEL: Is he all right?

JAKEY: Leo! Wake up!
(*Beat.*) Leo! Come on, what's the matter with you?

Beat – MICHAEL and JAKEY look at each other. Suddenly LEO sits bolt upright.

LEO: (*Screaming his own name.*) Leo!

Everyone jumps.

LEO: What's going on? Where am I? Where are we?

JAKEY: Jesus!

MICHAEL: Come on then. Come on.

LEO: What's happening?

JAKEY: Nothing. You were asleep.

LEO: How long?

JAKEY: Five minutes.

LEO looks round the room.

LEO: I'm back *here* again.

JAKEY: We haven't left yet.

LEO: Still here.

JAKEY: (*Beat.*) Come on. Jerry's opening late.

LEO brushes down his face with his hand.

LEO: Something terrible's happened!

JAKEY: Nothing's happened Leo. It's fine.

LEO: I feel it. Something terrible.

MICHAEL: Off we go. Come on.

JAKEY: All right. Keep your hair on.

MICHAEL: (*Looking at his watch – panic.*) I mean…how long's it gonna take…

LEO: (*Doomy.*) To fix?

JAKEY: Not long.

MICHAEL: I should've come in earlier.

LEO: It's still not fixed.

MICHAEL looks at his watch.

MICHAEL: Like how long?

JAKEY: Half an hour. If we all muck in. (*HE LAUGHS.*)

MICHAEL: (*Calculating.*) Half an hour. Half an hour. (*He looks at his watch.*) All right. Change of plan. You do it. You two leave.

LEO: Me do it?

JAKEY: What?

MICHAEL: Yes. You two go.

He paces nervously.

JAKEY: How come we go?

MICHAEL: Whaddya want? A room here? You're done. Come on.
All right Leo?

LEO: Of course.

JAKEY: Hold up. He can't do it on his own.

MICHAEL: Course he can. You can't you.

LEO: Could I have a drink of water?

MICHAEL: (*To JAKEY.*) He's fine.

JAKEY: He's asking you for water Michael?

MICHAEL: Do you want to start packing?

JAKEY: Get him some water Bizzy.

MICHAEL: I'll *get* him some water. (*ie, in a minute.*)

MICHAEL goes to JAKEY's belongings.

This your stuff.

JAKEY: Leave that.

MICHAEL: Come on, it's late.

JAKEY walks out purposefully.

MICHAEL: Leo?
(*LEO stares.*) I just don't want him here?

LEO: Fine.

MICHAEL: I want him out, soon as possible. Nothing
personal. I'll give you a bonus. You can do it on your
own can't you.

LEO: Of course.

Enter JAKEY with water.

JAKEY: There y'are Leo.

MICHAEL: Okay, so that's decided. Leo's going to fix the
electrics, the two of you can leave.
Thanks so much boys. And thanks for the advice earlier.

JAKEY: Just wanted to see her face, her reaction.

MICHAEL: I'm sorry. You can't.

JAKEY: All this time here.

MICHAEL: (*To BIZZY.*) Pack your things up. You're leaving.

JAKEY: Why Michael?

MICHAEL: Because I said so.

JAKEY: Don't you trust me?

MICHAEL: Not one bit.

JAKEY: You're worried I might say something.

LEO scratches his head tiredly.

MICHAEL: There's something you want. I don't know what it is. I don't *care* what it is. I just want you to go.

JAKEY: Not my fault she changed her mind Michael.

MICHAEL: Leo, do me a favour, send your boys home will you.

LEO lumbers to life, but it's rather slow and MICHAEL sees ahead.

LEO: No problem Michael. No problem at all. I don't know why we're all getting so hot under the collar.

Beat.

MICHAEL: Better idea. Why don't you all go.

LEO: No but…

MICHAEL: Yes. The room looks perfect. Really perfect.
And quiet too. It's a wonderful Quiet Space.
Just a silly little wire. Really. You've done wonderful work.
Everyone's tired. Go home.

He takes some notes out his pocket and pushes them into LEO's hand.

There you are. Have a drink on me.

LEO: Thank you. That's very kind but…

MICHAEL: I'll have someone fix it tomorrow. It's not a problem.

LEO: (*Affably.*) …see, there's really no need.

MICHAEL: Look at you. You're exhausted. All of you. Go and have a drink. Go on. Thank you. Thanks so much for your work.

He extends his hand which LEO then shakes.

LEO: But it's really no trouble for us to fix the…

MICHAEL: (*Bawling at LEO.*) If I want someone else to fix the wire, is that not my own damned business!

He releases LEO's hand. LEO pulls away, staring at MICHAEL.

LEO: What's going on? I don't understand. I'm sorry. I'm lost. Have I skipped a page?

MICHAEL: (*Empathy.*) Leo Leo Leo.
You're a good man.

LEO: Just half an hour, that's/ all it'll take…

MICHAEL: (*Still faux jovial.*) Honestly, it's fine.

LEO: (*At his mildest.*) It really would mean so much if you'd just allow me to finish the job.

MICHAEL: (*Enraged.*) Will you listen to me you dim fat fuck! I want you out this building immediately. Don't you get it?

Beat – LEO's shocked face makes MICHAEL more angry.

Fuck the fucking wire! Fuck it! I couldn't give a fuck about the fucking wire! I just want you to fucking evaporate! Now!

Pause. MICHAEL puts his hand to his head and recovers himself.

I'm so sorry.

He goes into his pocket again.

Really, I'm so sorry.

Exit MICHAEL. Quickly enters again with money.

Look. Please. Have a meal. On me. A nice one. All of you. Enjoy yourselves. I'm so sorry. I'm so tense and so sorry and so ridiculous.
I don't know where I am with this woman. Since her fucking mother…you know…I'm just…I'm such a mess. I'm jealous. I'm not thinking straight. Three months I've been waiting for her.
All afternoon in that room surrounded by her aromas. It said nothing about this in *Cosmopolitan.*

Shrugs. LEO stares and then acts with as much solemn dignity as he can muster.

LEO: Thank you Michael. I don't need the money. (*He returns the cash.*)

MICHAEL: Oh come on.

LEO: I may have my faults, but a dim fat fuck I am not.

MICHAEL: I'm so sorry.

LEO: I'm an hard-working man. Rich people sometimes get funny ideas about hard-working men. (*Beat.*) Right then lads.

MICHAEL: I'm really so sorry.

LEO goes to fetch his tool bag as if he were laying a wreath at the cenotaph.
Poignant. Lovely.
JAKEY and BIZZY stare then follow his lead.

JAKEY: You're right Leo. You don't have to take that. Leave him to it.

LEO comes to the door. He turns back to survey the room.

LEO: Good job of work that lads. A grand job of work. Done yourselves proud.

He nods at MICHAEL, saying his name.

Michael.

And out he trundles, followed by JAKEY and BIZZY. As BIZZY walks past, he delivers…

BIZZY: Tosser.

And they're gone.
MICHAEL shuts the door behind them.

MICHAEL: I'm so sorry.

He stands alone in the quiet space, leaning back against the door, breathing. And then he smiles. He hears a car outside and goes to the window, sees KATHERINE arriving.

MICHAEL: Oh God.

Immediately he starts scurrying around. He smells his armpits. He switches on the fountains. Tidies the remains of the 'danger zone.'
The door opens. MICHAEL is the other side of the room when KATHERINE comes in. In she walks. Her face has opened. She has lost that enveloping tension. MICHAEL stares at her fiercely. Hotly. Lustfully. She looks at him, and then surveys her perfect room from the door.)

KATHERINE: (*Langorous.*) My oh my.

MICHAEL just stares, breathing hard. She closes the door without turning back to it.

KATHERINE: My oh my.

She looks around the room again, then fixes on MICHAEL and smiles.

KATHERINE: So quiet.

MICHAEL stares.

When did they leave?

MICHAEL: A short while ago.

Beat.

KATHERINE: Hello.

MICHAEL: Hello Katherine.

KATHERINE: Long time.

MICHAEL: Yes. A long time.

They stare – electricity in the air.

KATHERINE: Someone's been hard at it.

MICHAEL smiles. She walks round trailing her hand over the newness.

Thank you.

MICHAEL stares.

It's beautiful.

She walks over to him, loosening and shedding clothes, in complete control.

KATHERINE: They wouldn't listen to me. (*Beat.*) Had to bring in my sheriff.

She comes to him and starts to unbutton his shirt.

MICHAEL: Katherine. Are you back?

He tries to touch her. She pushes his hands away.

KATHERINE: Aren't they funny. Men. They listen to the sheriff.

She starts kissing his chest.

What a strange and complicated summer it's been. Do you know, I think I might be.
Back.

KATHERINE kisses his neck.

Such a beautiful room.

He wants to embrace her but she pushes his arms away roughly.

Just starting to feel myself again now. Skins slipping away.

She slips onto her knees in front of him.

MICHAEL: Wonderful news.

She presses her face against his groin.

KATHERINE: I'm sorry I've had to keep you so far away from me. You've been very good.
(*Beat.*) Very good. (*Beat.*) I thought about you today.
Waiting. Longing. Patient. Decent.
Have I been unbearable?

MICHAEL: You have been.

KATHERINE: I thought so. These last weeks. They've just been a blur.
I'm sorry.
(*Beat.*) I wonder how I'll make it up to you.

He puts his hands on her head, but she resists firmly and immediately. MICHAEL feels a frisson.

I'm glad to know I can trust you.

MICHAEL: Yes.

KATHERINE: I was worried that perhaps it was just heat. Electricity. Between us. We need more than that.

Beat.

If you're to be allowed into my secret places.

She stands and moves round the room.

KATHERINE: What a wonderful room. I feel so light in here. Like I could just float into the air and out the window.

MICHAEL steps forward.

MICHAEL: I want you so completely.

KATHERINE straight back to earth, fixes him and halts him.

KATHERINE: I know you do.

MICHAEL: Yes.

KATHERINE: I think it's time I left mummy behind. She wants me to be happy. I felt it so much today. After that storm. Being with people. Walking in here now. Everything seems so clear.

MICHAEL: I'm glad.

KATHERINE: Can you forgive me?

MICHAEL: Always.

MICHAEL: God Katherine!

He pulls her roughly into him kissing her and throws her against the wall.
The door opens. Enter, unseen, JAKEY.
He coughs, they spring apart. KATHERINE starts laughing.

MICHAEL: Jesus Christ!

JAKEY: So sorry. Sorry Michael.

KATHERINE: I don't believe it.

MICHAEL: What do you want?

JAKEY: Sorry
(*To KATHERINE.*) Hello. How do you like it? Is it what you wanted?

MICHAEL: What are you doing!

But KATHERINE is in light spirits. She starts giggling.

KATHERINE: Oh God. You've come back.
(*Giggling.*) Of course you have. How could you not?

JAKEY: Sorry.

KATHERINE: It's wonderful. It really is. I'm so sorry. About everything. I feel...positively drunk in here...

JAKEY: Great. Result.

MICHAEL: Get out!

KATHERINE: Oh Michael.

JAKEY: I will I will.

MICHAEL: Now! Get out!

JAKEY: I will. Sorry. It's the boy. He's lost a button. A little button on his Walkman. You know. Tiny rubber thing.

MICHAEL: Jesus Christ!

JAKEY: He's going on and on. He won't let us leave. You know how kids are. (*Beat.*) Maybe not.

MICHAEL: Out. Now!

JAKEY: Can't I just have a look? Two minutes. It'll make things much easier for me.

MICHAEL interposes to prevent JAKEY entering.

MICHAEL: I said out! Now!

KATHERINE: Michael. Come on sweetheart. Two minutes.

JAKEY: He's everso upset?

MICHAEL: What's the matter with you?

KATHERINE: (*Mollifying.*) Come on Michael. He's forgotten something. It's comical.

MICHAEL: No.

She stands and goes to him, rubs his shoulders, kisses him.

KATHERINE: Michael.

Kissing his neck from the back.

Let him have a look. It's all right. Hmm? Let him look for his little button. (*She gets a fit of the giggles.*)

MICHAEL: (*Breaking loose and flashing eyes at her.*) For Christ's sake, haven't you had your fill of each other these past seventeen bloody weeks!

KATHERINE looks, and her smile fades to disappointment.

KATHERINE: I'm going to have a shower.

She walks out passing between the two men. Frisson.

MICHAEL: Katherine.

JAKEY: Thanks. (*To MICHAEL.*) Sorry. (*He shrugs.*) She'll be all right.

He enters.

Silly thing to lose. Shouldn't come off. Badly made see.

MICHAEL: (*Eyes narrowing.*) A tiny rubber button.

JAKEY: Yeah.

Just a…tiny little knob. (*Beat.*) But so important. (*They stare, then, indicating in KATHERINE'S direction.*) What a difference a day makes. (*Beat.*) Sexy girl. I forgot.

MICHAEL stares.

(Beat.) I'll have a little look then. That all right?

JAKEY wanders round the room seeking this button. MICHAEL shadows him impatiently.

MICHAEL: You think I'm stupid?

JAKEY: 'scuse me?

MICHAEL: There's no button.

JAKEY: Should be somewhere.

JAKEY searches.

MICHAEL: Kept it in for three months. All bottled up. One little slip, the smile's off her face. Three months I waited for that smile.

JAKEY searches.

JAKEY: Glad she likes the room. I'll tell Leo. He'll be everso pleased.

MICHAEL stares.

MICHAEL: What do you want? Why are you here?

JAKEY: I'm looking for the button. The little thing. I told you.

Searches. MICHAEL starts circling. Sound of shower, sound of water in the room.

MICHAEL: You wanna embarrass me? Humiliate me? That it?

JAKEY: You need any help?

JAKEY searches.

MICHAEL: There's no button.

JAKEY: Kids. Luck of the draw I get Bizzy.
(*Stands.*) I mean, they're all a pain in the bloody arse but he's in a league of his own. What he puts me through.

JAKEY returns to his foraging. MICHAEL paces round him like a cat watching a hedgehog.

MICHAEL: The mother run off did she? Eh? Mother run off and leave you?

JAKEY: She weren't ever really with me to be honest Michael.

MICHAEL stares.

MICHAEL: That's funny you want to do that. One life and you want to do that with it.

JAKEY hunts.

Different world. All that messed up family stuff. Finishes you off before you've even started. Not for me. I don't want that. I make a decision, I stick to it.

JAKEY: Trouble is, it's her as well isn't it.

Beat – MICHAEL inward.

She's looking nice. More like she was the start of the Summer.

Pause.

MICHAEL: Listen. There's nothing I don't know about Katherine. We have no secrets.
We're together. I know now.

Beat.

JAKEY: Yeah well. There's always a door they can walk out of. Any time.
That's why I don't bother with it no more.

Pause. MICHAEL walks out in a fury. Beat. Walks back in.

MICHAEL: What are you after? (*Beat.*) There's no button. The whole thing's a charade. What do you want?

Beat.

I spoke freely. I gave you *information.* About me and Katherine.

Pause – then strong…

I don't know what sort of Voodoo you used to twist it out of me.

Pause.

What are you doing here? You wanna turn that against me.
What is it you want? Money? I won't give you money. You? Look at you. You're fit for nothing. You're a layabout. Bloody layabout you! Three months to build this crap? (*JAKEY looks up.*) Oh make no mistake, it's shit. It'll be down in three weeks. Now she's back to normal. (*Beat.*) Three months for this garbage? How d'you get out of bed in the morning? I bet you live in filth. You. Filth. With your football and your bloody satellite dish and your phone-ins and your opinions out of little newspapers.
Get out!
(*Beat.*) I said get out of here!
Now!

Enter KATHERINE in bath robe. Silence.

KATHERINE: Not found it?

JAKEY: Not yet.

KATHERINE: That's a pity.

She comes in and has a brief look around. MICHAEL and JAKEY stare.

KATHERINE: Look at this room. I can't quite believe it. This is my house. Thank you. Thank you so much.

JAKEY: That's all right. (*Beat.*) Just sorry we took so long.

KATHERINE: (*Lightening.*) Well I'm sorry I blew a fuse the way I did.

JAKEY: Caw dear oh dear. There you go again. Apologising.

KATHERINE: (*Coy.*) Whoops. I know.

JAKEY: Gotta stop with that.

KATHERINE: Sorry.

JAKEY: Just say what you like darlin'. You bottle too much up. It's not good for you. Let it all come out. There's nothing to be afraid of in life. Absolutely nothing.

KATHERINE: No. There isn't.

JAKEY: You see.

KATHERINE: Look at this room. It's so light. So positive. Mummy would have loved it. With the beautiful tree. Mummy loved that tree.

She spies something on the floor.

What's that? Look. Is that it?

KATHERINE picks up a little rubber button. She holds it up to the light.

Look Michael. A tiny little button. Look at that, see. 'Play'. Is that it?

JAKEY: That's it. That's why he wanted it. It was the *play* button. Must've come off.

KATHERINE: Isn't that funny. Did you see? The moment I mentioned 'mummy' we found it. (*Beat. She hovers round the room.*) The very moment. That's good. That's a very good sign. She's happy.

She puts the little button in JAKEY's hand. He closes his hand over hers.

JAKEY: She's given you her blessing. Well. Bye darlin'. No hard feelings eh. You take care of yourself.

She stares at him just a moment too long and then takes her hand away somewhat flushed.
Enter LEO.

KATHERINE: (*Still light.*) Oh look. They're all coming back!

MICHAEL: Oh my God.

LEO: Oh hello love. Sorry love. Don't want to disturb you my darling. Nothing of the sort sweetheart. So sorry lover. It's Jakey I'm after. (*He nods at MICHAEL.*) Michael.

MICHAEL: Jesus Fucking Christ!

KATHERINE: Michael. Don't worry. Please. Don't worry.

LEO stares uncomfortably.

Leo. (*KATHERINE goes and kisses him on the forehead.*) Thank you for the work you've done on my home. It's beautiful.

MICHAEL: Oh my God!

LEO: Well thank you sweetheart. Thank you lover.

KATHERINE giggles at him.

LEO: So kind. Kind words.

KATHERINE: (*Through giggles.*) I'm glad I got the chance to tell you.

LEO: Thank you sweetheart. Thank you love.

He's itching to communicate with JAKEY.

KATHERINE: Really. It's wonderful. Thank you both. I have to...

She points out her robe.

JAKEY: (*Charming.*) Course darling.

LEO: I'm so glad. Everso pleased.

Exit KATHERINE.

Everso sorry. Sorry Michael. Just a quick one.
(*Beat – to JAKEY.*) It's Bizzy? Have you seen him?

Pulling JAKEY out his reverie.

JAKEY: I thought he was with you.

LEO: He was, but he's gone.

JAKEY: Whaddya mean gone?

LEO: He's gone. He's disappeared.

JAKEY: Disappeared where?

LEO: I don't know. I was in a daze. I thought he was in the back. He must have slipped off.

MICHAEL hunts round the room foaming with anger.

MICHAEL: Disappeared has he? Perhaps he's somewhere in the room. Let me have a look? No, I can't seem to find him. Wait, fallen into the fountain has he? No, not there either. Hang on, stuck behind the Elephant God Ganesh is he? No. Or perhaps he's been miniaturized and we're trampling him to death under our very feet.

(*He lifts his shoe.*) No. Well then. (*Shouting.*) Perhaps you'd be better off looking for him outside this fucking flat and leaving us in peace!

JAKEY: He probably went to the shop.

LEO: I had a look there see…

From next door, KATHERINE screams. The men start. Look at each other.

MICHAEL: Katherine! Katherine!

KATHERINE runs into the Quiet Space.

MICHAEL: What's the matter? What is it?

KATHERINE: (*Catching her breath.*) There's someone… there's someone in my room.

MICHAEL: What?

KATHERINE: In my cupboard. When I opened it! He was there. Oh God.

MICHAEL: Who? Who's there Katherine?

JAKEY: Oh Christ.

JAKEY looks at LEO.
Enter BIZZY. Frightened. His top off, wearing it round his waist, his trousers tellingly loose, but almost a subliminal detail.

BIZZY: Wanted to give her key back. I had it you see.

JAKEY: Bizzy.

BIZZY: Just wanted to give the key back, that's all. Honest.

Freeze, then MICHAEL runs at him.

MICHAEL: You little bastard!

MICHAEL Dives on top of BIZZY.

JAKEY: Wait. Wait no. Michael.

MICHAEL trying to land a good punch on BIZZY.

MICHAEL: What were you doing in there little bastard!

KATHERINE: Michael!

JAKEY steps in to try and pull MICHAEL off.

LEO: No. Boys. That's not the way!

JAKEY: Get off him. (*Beat.*) Leave him alone.

BIZZY wriggles away but MICHAEL and JAKEY bind together and wrestle around the room.

KATHERINE: No. Stop it. Please. Michael. Stop it.

Into the wall go JAKEY and MICHAEL – damage.

KATHERINE: No!

Into the fountain. Damage. The elephant. Damage.
Men locked together. The fountains have collapsed and are leaking onto the floor.

KATHERINE: Please. No. Stop it! Mummy! Make them stop!

BIZZY goes to the wire and pulls it away from the wall, like a hose. Not seen.

BIZZY: Shall I get him dad. Up his Khyber.

LEO looks up.

LEO: No Bizzy!

BIZZY pushes the wire onto MICHAEL – JAKEY sees it when it's too late.

JAKEY: Bizzy! No! Conduction Bizzy! Conduction!

JAKEY tries to wriggle away but the shock passes through MICHAEL and JAKEY.

They both drop down stunned as if dead.
BIZZY stares.
LEO stares. BIZZY smiles at LEO. A strange moment of
quiet.

LEO: Conduction Bizzy see. Conduction.

There is water pouring onto the floor and the wire is dangling
down as BIZZY holds it.
BIZZY stares at KATHERINE.

LEO: Best not go near them just now sweetheart.
Health and safety. Won't be as serious as it looks, don't
you worry.
I'll get the electricity off. That all right with you love?

KATHERINE nods.

Hang onto that wire Bizzy. Just like that son, don't let it
drop, good lad.
Minor repairs. Nothing serious. We can come by next
week, put it to rights.
Won't be two ticks.

Exit LEO. BIZZY, still staring at KATHERINE. He smiles.

BIZZY: Dad said you have to get a girl to tell you her
secrets if you want them to fall in love with you and he
said I shouldn't of read your book.
I know I shouldn't of, but it was the best book I ever
ever read because it was all about you an' that's the only
book I want to read.
Honest!

Beat – KATHERINE stares.

'July the twenty second. Builders seem slow. Couldn't
concentrate. Noise, endless noise. Terrible feeling in the
pit of my stomach. Michael rings and rings. Wants to see
me. He understands nothing. He's shallow. Perhaps I
need someone shallow. Thinking about sex all the time.

Not with Michael. He repulses me. Is that wrong? I suppose I'd get used to it. Women do. Self-centred, up and down.

KATHERINE: (*Half-hearted and quiet.*) Stop.

BIZZY: Arranged to meet Cassian in Denmark Street. Will go when the builders have gone. Of course he'll want to fuck me. Who cares. Let him. His flat stinks of cats. That guy Davies still thinks he can have me whenever he clicks his fingers. At least he's handsome. Not like Gary. God listen to me. Gary who? I don't even know. He didn't even use protection. I don't care. Is it wrong? Excited now thinking of him. I should tell Michael. Where would I start. Poor Michael. Poor over-excited Michael. He'll never understand. What am I doing? It's not me. It's not me...'

KATHERINE: No.

BIZZY stops. He stares at KATHERINE.

BIZZY: See, I can keep it all secret for you. I can. I can.

BIZZY stares at KATHERINE, makes a decision, grits his teeth and touches the cable, but it's harmless now.
Enter LEO.

LEO: All right lads. Let's go then shall we? Jakey?

LEO goes and helps JAKEY stagger up from the back.

JAKEY: Thanks Leo.

BIZZY: (*Laughing.*) Feels funny don't it dad.

JAKEY: Yeah. Yeah it does.

BIZZY: Don't matter if it makes you impotent does it. Cause you got me already.

BIZZY helps JAKEY and LEO to the door.

JAKEY: Bizzy son...make no mistake, you got funny ways...and God knows life's gonna be one long hard uphill struggle...but I like you. I like you son.

BIZZY beams. JAKEY puts his arm round him.

BIZZY: Got it up his Khyber.

JAKEY: You did didn't you.
(*Beat.*) And I got your button.

BIZZY: Lovely.

JAKEY: Lovely

And BIZZY and JAKEY leave.

LEO: (*To KATHERINE.*) So glad you liked the work. Glad you approved. (*Beat.*) We'll put this right. Don't you worry. We can come back next week. After that, it may be difficult. Busy time of year see.

Beat.

Right ho then. Cheerio. All the best.
Ba-bye.

Exits.

MICHAEL: (*Weakly.*) Katherine?

KATHERINE: I'm sorry.

Black.